modern

Prose Poems

1987-2007

history

modern
Christopher Buckley
1987-2007
Prose Poems
history

TUPELO PRESS

Modern History: Prose Poems 1987-2007

Copyright © 2008 Christopher Buckley

ISBN-978-1-932195-68-2

LCCN: 2008926705

First paperback edition October 2008

Tupelo Press

PO Box 539, Dorset, Vermont 05251

802.366.8185 • Fax 802.362.1883

www.tupelopress.org

Cover painting, *Untitled*, by Richard Silva

COVER AND TEXT DESIGN BY HOWARD KLEIN

Tupelo Press is an award-winning independent literary press that publishes fine fiction,
non-fiction and poetry in books that are as much a joy to hold as they are to read.
Tupelo Press is a registered 501(c)3 non-profit organization and relies on donations to
carry out its mission of publishing extraordinary works of literature that may be outside
the realm of large commercial publishers.

"By definition, a government has no conscience. Sometimes it has a policy, but nothing more."

—*Albert Camus*

"But home is the form of the dream, & not the dream."

—*Larry Levis*

Contents

III

Introduction

Reading Christopher Buckley's *Modern History, Prose Poems 1987–2007*, it is impossible not to think of Walt Whitman's famous dictum: "Comerado! This is no book;/Who touches this touches a man." *Modern History* is Buckley's most personal book to date. In no other work is his presence so immediate and unmediated. The extravagant lyricism, the questing intelligence, the spiritual longing, the honesty and the zany humor that mark his many previous books are all at play here, but it is the implied, "Comerado," that sets this book apart. Addressing directly any companionable soul who might stumble upon them, these poems offer pleasures to anyone with an appetite for delight.

Modern History makes it clear that Buckley is disinterested in parsing the petty distinctions between genres. Like Marcel Duchamp who declared that his ready-mades were, in fact, sculptures, Buckley insists (and he has no time to argue) that his prose poems are poems—because he says they are. This is not a petty distinction. Many of Buckley's prose poems are poems by default. Neither essays nor short stories, neither social commentary nor scientific inquiry, neither critique, dissertation nor philosophical discourse, his prose poems are all of these and more. Only the authority of an impulsive poetic voice could animate poems of such range and depth. Certainly Buckley has the poetic credentials. The much praised, award-winning author of 16 volumes of verse, Buckely has published memoirs, anthologies and a slew of critical books as well; he's proven himself to be a master of many genres. His prose poems stretch the boundaries of the form, but they persistently ask us—and this is part of their power and their charm—what else could they be?

Christopher Buckley is a modern day schoolman, parsing both heaven and earth to get a closer look at the absolute. As comfortable with quantum theory as he is with the catechism or classic cars, his real project is to rescue time, to redeem the past from the erosion of memory and the crushing wheel of history. In prose poems roaring with more energy than the teenage companions who often serve as Greek chorus to his universal Everyman, Buckley luxuriates in "the jackpot of lingo" offered up by science, religion, pop culture and sports. He mines the lyrical residue of his age—Simonized Chryslers, Gina Lollobrigida, doo-wop and Brylcreem—for his libretto to a celestial music that defies the passing years. Avuncular, knowing, generous and humane, Christopher Buckley carries the reader along in unstinting pursuit of his "moon-bright, night-blind youth." In his poem, *Eternity*, Buckley thanks God "for the gift of the eccentric brain," and for the "moonraking poem which keeps me alive in prayer." Amen to that.

For all the warmth, nostalgia and generosity of spirit, there is a strain of righteous anger animating much of this book. Buckley takes on corrupt politicians, the cultural elite, the academy and corporate malefactors with an equal measure of rage and resignation. Buckley never advocates any particular political party or philosophic or economic system, but he throws his weight unfailingly against oppression. He lowers his lance against pretension and greed, and he rebels against the small, unnecessary cruelties that tip the world toward darkness. For Buckley, all history is personal history. In *Patriot Act*, he draws the connection between a piece of corrosive legislation and "some worthless SOB" who cuts down the trees along his back fence. *Modern History* begins innocently enough with children enjoying a double feature at the theatre, but it suddenly ricochets from Nagasaki to the Depression, past Churchill and Stalin to JFK and the grassy knoll, with stop-overs in Bosnia, Birkenau, and "the failure at Thermopylae as well." Buckley has taken notes, and he's naming names.

No rant or screed, even one with which we agree, will hold our interest for long without some leavening, and Buckley's preferred ingredient is humor. With perfect comedic timing, he riffs like a jazzman, throwing out one-liners, and then racing through an avalanche of word play, puns and jokes. *Oil, Nostalgia, Immigration Reform, & the Decline of the West*—as ponderous a title as one is likely to find in a book of poems—begins: "All right, geniuses, what do you expect?" and Buckley is off to the races. *My History of Ancient Egypt*, a tour de force that merges history, religion, Hollywood and the poet's old girlfriends evolves into a mytho-poetic sermon on mortality, which ends with "Yul Brynner on TV doing a commercial for The National Cancer Society...more serious and earnest than he'd ever been, after he was dead."

Buckley's wit is biting at times, but never cruel, and more often than not he turns his humor on himself. This imbues his poems with a disarming modesty, and his self-deprecation makes it clear that he's in on the joke. You want to believe a man who declares, "I have a graduate degree in vagary." In *Buckley y yo*, his send-up of Borges, he admits, "I'm busy reading a little philosophy, dumbed-down books on astrophysics, though no one ever asks me what I know about gravity or the afterlife." Suffering through a low-carb diet, he complains, "These days, it's all fishes, no loaves," and he begins *My 25th Guggenheim Application* with, "I'm nothing, if not persistent."

Although it's tempting to read *Modern History* as an entertaining compendium of nostalgic detail and a fascinating primer of scientific advances, it is much more than that. Humor and verbal pyrotechnics aside, the real subject of *Modern History* is eschatology. Having reached an age when "death is no longer some distant city off in the analogical hills," Buckley sees the end drawing near and hopes "there is some there, there—beyond the clouds, the waves, the shadows on the empty surface of the sea." A skilled raconteur, Buckley often beguiles his readers with an amusing anecdote or a farcical yarn, and though we may applaud his description of a fish-tailing '59 Chevy Biscayne, the real subject is "Death as he rode next to me each day as I drove the foothills."

Buckley surveys the world, and in every detail he catches a glimpse of the absolute, a thread on some celestial loom that shuttles between the arcane minutia of his everyday life and the cosmic progression of the spheres. Buckley sees the sublime in the quotidian, and so the recitation of those sublime moments spent surfing, listening to Duane Eddy, wrecking a car, watching a movie or listening to the birds become a secular catechism. "I'm no longer even a Romantic," he admits in *Infinity*, "and know enough to mistrust the sweetness of the world." Of course it is just this sweetness that seduces him again and again, and feeds his hunger for the absolute, for reconciliation with the God of the sparrows, the ocean and the clouds. Buckley never succumbs to despair, but he asks, "What language can we finally aspire to beyond the cold Esperanto of the stars?"

Buckley's nostalgia then is not the typical longing for a lost ideal, but rather for a true Eden. Santa Barbara "and the creamy, book-perfect, fair-weather clouds of the '50s going over the Figueroa range—since the age of 4, the clouds and trees carrying off my thoughts…" He attempts to reclaim these drifting thoughts, these childish reveries, "letting my blood download its indiscriminate freight, making some lighter sense of things doing no more finally than it seems I ever should have in the first place." With God missing or aloof, Buckley looks for "substitutions in the sky," and so the clouds, the salt spray and his own breath propel him toward an ineluctable but unfathomable end.

"Turning 59" begins, "Now I can nag the stars with impunity, because, Why Not?" Age has released the poet from anxiety, and though still suspicious of his own mind, Buckley admits that, "No matter what we formulate, we spend our lives here in hope, or in refusing it." Simultaneously relaxed and passionate, searching and skeptical, his poems mine the past for hints about a future that may only lead to oblivion, but a future he has faith in nonetheless. When Buckley says, "I love each deep breath I take here, away from everything, love looking up along side the pomegranates and pittosporum, the ornamental plum," we believe him in our bones. If there is a poet writing in America today with a bigger heart, I'd like to meet him.

—*Gary Young*

1

Eternity (being a condensed spiritual and aesthetic biography)

for VS

No one says I look 55—no one says I don't, except my new friend Virgil. He has two catholic daughters and like me, hates to fly, but there's no other way to get home in time for the youngest's 1st Communion. I almost remember mine…I've been scared ever since—of Death, of course. You tell me why…. In 2nd grade, the nun lectured us about Eternity, which almost arrived later from Cuba in the early '60s, Cuba where my friend Virgil was born, which has at least one entrance to hell and exits in Spain and L.A. In the afterlife, I don't think anyone is rolling cigars while someone reads them *Don Quixote* in the original. Anyway, we were going to spend Eternity in hell if we did not do as we were told. Sister explained that Eternity was like an enormous steel ball, the size of the earth, upon which an eagle, gliding in from the cosmic starry dark beyond Cleveland and the east coast, once every million years, landed and took off again. The time it took that steel ball to completely wear away from the friction of the eagle landing and lifting away was less than a second of Eternity, the time we'd be burning on a hot rock for cussing, eating hot dogs on Fridays, not making our yearly Easter obligation of communion and mass, or having impure thoughts about Belinda Sanchez. Go figure.

What if, on the practical side, the universe—and so time-space—does curve back on itself like a huge quesadilla? We're going nowhere. What, then, have we been suffering for all along? More specifically, what have I been doing with that image like a fish hook in my brain for 48 years? Nuns, with their psycho-spiritual hammer-locks, were terrorists, and they did not discriminate among ages or ethnic groups. Death, darkness, and sure damnation were there equally for us all if we didn't stop talking during mass and go out and finagle quarters from relatives and folks on our block for the pagan babies. Dear God.

I don't know what angel brings me these lines in the middle of the night after I'm up and down the hall to the bathroom, brings them every few years like a palm tree and a pool of water appearing after sands have shifted for no reason, like some metaphysical crust of light. Some angel sweeping down with dust, one in the back of the chorus singing hosannas like nobody's business who has a little time to spare, an angel who every now and then hands off a few imagistic granules while I'm flaming away here in the flesh, in darkness where I might not know the source but would know a gift when I heard one.

Once I'm half awake and the cells are ticking over like new stars, I lose track of time and switch the lamp on and off and write down phrases, losing sleep—what does it come to? The door of a '59 Chevy swings open like a vault and lets out some earlier, more sprightly version of me, only a few blocks from happiness, or the sea, which ever comes first—with my papers and a new poem in hand—more than I arrived with. Who knew where I was headed? The nuns were sure: Hell. Virgil and I voted for Spain, even southern California if that's the best we could do to breathe cool salt air. Maybe I could do this forever, who knows? As I was taught, worse things could happen to me. Outside of Time, will poems matter? Why ask now—I'm not an academic, an administrator, slick in a Republican suit. We're not for long, not forever. Death, of course. And next? I hope it's not hell, or anywhere near Pennsylvania, where I already served ten years for my sins.

Dear God. Thank you for the gift of the eccentric brain, this associative jelly. Thank you for this moonraking poem which keeps me alive in prayer, in doubt, and in hope. This poem which for once did not take 5 months and 50 drafts, though I would have waited patiently as always—like salt dissolving from the sea, like air gathering to be somewhere else, like the last flake of rust outside of time....

Les Etoiles

The school I'm sent to claims a hilltop on the other side of town. At night, the high surrounding house lights splash on and sparkle silver as anything in the sky. Each morning, royal palms ignite along the drive with waxy spikes of sun as we step off the bus by the courtyard for the lower grades. Pines and monkey puzzle trees swim dark as seaweed up the long blue air, and we're still so new that a day is a mysterious ordeal. We believe most anything we're shown, from the flames and thorns crowing Jesus' Sacred Heart to the big Dipper spilling out the Milky Way, or bread-crumbs left in the night sky by children who've wandered too far from home.... We're taught by nuns from France, and the task before us is to count, without the aid of our small star-white hands, backwards from 100 to 1. But having memorized my lesson and correctly pronounced, *Le livre est sur lat table, La fenetre est ouverte, Les etoiles sont dans le ciel*, I blank out having blown all the kilowatts at my command, and face the vast blackboard, a cosmos of numbers whirling inside my head....

Like the sky above the hills, our uniforms are midnight blue, pressed shirts white as clouds. During lunch we race recklessly about as the jays we resemble—Bill Kiley's in love with Mary Kay, and they're the brains in class, subtracting and adding numbers like there's no tomorrow. I'm running around after Leslie Baldwin who one day on the bus holds her binder up to block the driver's view and kisses me, her light blue eyes shimmering with that gloss in the windy sky.

The sky holds still, clouds and stars move overhead, I move around below, and a few years later I'm a guest at a club, her doubles partner, and though I serve well and we win, she vanishes into a crowd of shining tennis whites. Two more years and boys from our prep school (where I'll be withdrawn for back tuition) are bused to town. In crew cuts, tab collars and sport coats from J.C. Penney's, we're let out at the Baldwin's ranch-style home where Leslie fox trots in an amber floor-length gown in the arms of boys in dinner jackets and black bow ties, who talk of speed boats and beach clubs in Marina del Rey. (Ten years later, I'll catch a last glimpse of her in a galaxy of lace on the Society Page of the *Times*, married in a Beverly Hills hotel.)

For now, Kiley's here, still a brain, and I ask what we should do—

neither of us recognize the girls clustered in groups, nor do we dance well. We take our Dixie Cups of Hawaiian Punch and step out to the patio where he lights up a Newport behind the pepper tree. I cover for him, and while he cautiously exhales, I look up at light specks trailing off the winter branches into an incalculable sky, and think back years, how smart he was in arithmetic, how many stars—green, red, and gold—always glistened across his white shirt, how we all wished for stars to mark the brilliance of our days. I was awarded two that year and both for French, remember wandering dazzled about the schoolyard after class, singing names of things *en Français*, enthralled with words whose sum total equaled beauty, and proved as bright, as true, as the blue and silver stars pasted on my stiff collar.

My History of Ancient Egypt

The short version arrived in 1956 from Cecil B. De Mille, with Chuck Heston in his grey beard looking like Michelangelo, which is to say Moses, which is Art History 101, which I learned much later. In any event, God's coppery-green smoke snaked down out of the inky night over Luxor and found Yul Brynner's son and Pharaoh-to-be in the arc-lit stone palace and smothered him without a sound in Technicolor.

The underclass greased the logs used to roll the pyramid stones, big as beer trucks, along the sandy streets, while Heston—due to some issues of class in connection to his birth—was demoted from the executive branch to dance in the mud pits and make bricks without straw. An administrative practice that quickly caught on.

There was a silent release in black&white, filmed near my home, in the Guadalupe Dunes, in 1923, with the obelisks and great pillared halls, parapets and lines of house-sized lions raised before the sea, which, once the sun set on the lower kingdom, eventually drove the sands in the direction of the past, covering all the plaster feet of the gods. These were finally left to the domain of the sun and waves to break to bits not that long after the caravans of Hollywood caterers got their panel trucks stuck for the last time in the reedy creek crossing leading out of there.

The re-release of *The Ten Commandments* in 1965 was the last movie, I think, that my girlfriend and I ever saw together, and since we had read the book in grammar school and knew the ending, we walked out on Yvonne de Carlo, Heston, and the whole lot just after the red sea parted like two giant waves at Waimea cresting in a Bruce Brown surf movie. We sat in my '59 Chevy and had a fight, no doubt precipitated by her stern, pharaoh-like father with his all but shaved head and his dictates about how often we could date, and time limits talking on the phone. I'd learned nothing from the ancients and the lost civilizations of the sand that could help me there; in those days there were fewer places from which to summon plague on short order. For all I could see, the future looked like the past with improved transportation.

Later, one day in my mid 40s, I'd see Yul Brynner on TV doing a commercial for The National Cancer Society—I don't recall his surroundings—warning against smoking…more serious and earnest than he'd ever been, after he was dead.

Last Days of the Hot Rod Kids

Tuck Schneider, Fowler, Sozzi and me, thinking we were someone with Butch Wax, Brylcreem, Wild Root Cream Oil and more in our hair, whipped it into waves that peaked and never broke—flat tops, fenders, wings, waterfall spit curls in front—a glimmering, Doo Wap, quintessential sea of grease.

1950s, it was all you had—a republic of style, marshaled with nothing more than a comb. Freddy Canon, Fabian, and Fats Domino on record jackets, on Bandstand, studio lights rebounding off their high-rolling hair styles that had hardened into place— Elvis, on movie posters, on TV from the waist up. And if not them, then Tuck's big brother, Joe, going to Catholic High, wearing a red wind breaker Jimmy Dean wore in the movie as a first class juvenile delinquent, flipping a cigarette from the curb, blasting off in a hot rod Dodge. Joe would stop, spread his legs for balance, then pull a comb from his back pocket and make long, slow passes through the wings of this Duck-Tail to the point where they met in back of his head, to the point where he was suspended from school for three days, for such hair was dangerous stuff.

We were hip before the bell rang to line up by grades, arms'-distance apart, facing flag and crucifix, then we'd duck into the washroom to put parts on the left and mow down our jelly-rolled hoodlum hair, turn our collars back so we looked like the accountant's, farmer's, and Jr. Chamber of Commerce's sons we truly were.

And as soon as they boarded the bus, 8th grade girls popped open compacts and smeared on lipstick—blood-rose and tangerine—rolled up their uniform skirts to just below the knee which was where the House Un-American Activities Committee wanted to start investigating the subversive animal influence of Rock-n-Roll. Downtown, on sidewalks after school, they were sure they'd be taken for Judy Holliday, Gina Lollobrigida, or Sandra Dee, as they swayed down the streets in saddle shoes, confidently snapping their gum.

Last period study hall in the auditorium, with no clock, we'd listen for all 348 cubes of Louis De Ponce's metallic-green '58 Chevy bellowing up East Valley Road to tell us that soon we'd be let out and riding our ten-speeds over to Tuck's to play 45s of The Ventures, Duane Eddy and the Rebels, Jorgan Ingman—as much amplified Stratocastered twang as we could get at 99¢ + tax. And this would go on forever, or until the '60s and high school where class leaders were sheared by barbers who left "white sidewalls" above their ears, where they voluntarily wore suits and ties on test days, where nuns, priests, and Junior Achievement eliminated every black motorcycle jacket, chrome zipper, chain, slicked-back hair style from the scene. We joined Key Club, Lettermen's Club, fool-happy to set up chairs for assembly, to sell religious chocolate bars door to door. Never mind Kennedy, Peace Corps, and The New Frontier, our fathers of the merchant class were on the corporate golf course and would not cut Johnny Cool, Hey Daddy O, and low-riders in souped-up Chevys and Mercs any slack. No, we were all going to wear loafers, slacks, button-down shirts, and study Business Administration. James Dean had been T-boned in his Porsche outside Cholame and was a bit of blond dust over Hwy 41 and the past. Elvis was in the army with a buzz-cut like every other grunt.

And in their beehives and bouffants shining like chiffon, in their stiff dresses, who knew what mysteries girls were holding back? We had to put on business suits, tie thin ties through tab collars, and ask them to dance to a band sappy with trombones if we were going to find out. Chaperones scrutinized the space between us as we leaned into each other inch by inch in the dark, and only a few older ones took the path of least resistance out to the parking lot, ducking below the dash to avoid the flashlight of the padre on patrol.

1965, and Orsua and I had hair over our collars and were almost expelled. Half our generation would be hated for long hair and open opposition to the organizations of death. And though I'd studied French in grammar school, that was half my life ago, and I didn't know Dien Bien Phu from Doo Wha Diddy, Long Binh from Long Tall Sally. I didn't know that in no time Johnson and Westmorland would make skinheads and numbskulls of us all, send us to the end of our youth in the streets of Berkeley, Chicago, or Saigon without regard for who we were or might ever be, for the blood caked in body bags or in our unfashionable hair. And so haircut or not, it looked like I was headed for Canada, and nowhere fast.

There &Then

Though there's no going back, it happens all the time—sleep or daydreams, and I'm on the corner of State and Micheltorena, noon on a Saturday, the wide sidewalks shimmering with mica, Simonized Chryslers and Oldsmobiles, women with coral or ivory shopping bags sauntering in and out of I. Magnin, Lou Rose, as I wait for Slattery, Bolduc, and Schneider, the station wagons that will let them out and leave us on our own in all the world we know, seaside among white stucco and red tile roofs, a little principality of blue air and sun where someone with a dollar in change is free. Flipping 50¢ pieces, we strut with confidence into Woolworth's for M&Ms weighed-out by the pound and then head down to the California Theater on Canon Perdido, the last place where, still under 12, you get in for 15¢. No loges, a descending center aisle, and we sit in the cave-like glow in 1959, content to know almost nothing about our lives or what we're about to see despite a newsreel and our first year of Social Studies. We're happy, our hightop sneakers squeaking on the sticky floor, the freight of sugar so thoroughly embalming our veins that we're fairly oblivious to whatever Robert Mitchum and Yvonne De Carlo, Mel Ferrer and Joan Fontaine are up to.

We're supposed to be at the Arlington for cartoons, Audie Murphy and John Wayne, World War II again, where one dollar leaves us barely enough for Jujy Fruits or Junior Mints. So we opt for black & white, the burning silver profiles when someone's kissed. We can't tell Film Noir from Adult Romance, but guess what we see goes on somewhere in the world, though no one we know drinks martinis, flies to Mexico or Singapore. Four hours with previews and intermission—we exit walking slowly up the ramp in the building's shade before stepping out, almost blinded by the slant of winter light sharp as tin foil as we shield our eyes.

Next year, it's 50¢ for everyone, and we'll go there only one more time for *Alexander The Great* starring Richard Burton, something we think we'll understand—the spectacle and bloody Technicolor war. And though Alexander dies reasonably young at 32, that point in time floats out further than the ancient past. The rainbow of neon tubes hums on, the marquee fizzes and pops in the 5:00 dusk as I'm the last one to be picked up. When the doors close for good, I'll remember little about that battle for the civilized world raging all afternoon—I'll recall instead the face of Kim Novak, tragic and blond in a love scene as Kirk Douglas walked out on her a year or so before, and there and then think I know the complete depth and extent of loss, coming soon, out of the dark.

There

I've driven by a hundred times since the hundred times, early in the '60s, we parked along the shoreline for the twenty or thirty minutes of our permitted youth, our breath going nowhere beyond the steamed windshield glass...or the fog, which sometimes sauntered in from the dark and held us there with no idea where we really were…. I remember the great black cypress leaning on the grey-black sky, and the moon going to pieces in the eternal branches, the soporific salt air rising off the lines of surf that had us dreaming down hill in that same spot with a view toward nothing but ourselves, awaiting the acceptable sublime. Alone there, a car or two wandering by in the dim world forty years ago. The white background music of the tide, the crush of stars, clichés, and unclear wishes extended beyond our curfew and the days to come—unseeable then as the islands off the seabeach at night, where we were bound to the star-brocaded waves, the beach fires smoldering in the on-shore air…. Let me see now, let me see…what great thing was it I was going out into the world to do, prepared only with my haircut and button-down blue oxford, my night-blind youth, buoyed, like the moon, by vague love in the great vague sky where I claimed to read the sea-scrawl scraps of light by all the certainty we had coursing our salt-warm blood at seventeen?

Modern History

All of history is remorse.

—Carlos Drummond de Andrade

1959, and a squad of kids in someone's Ford Country Squire, dropped off at State and Victoria for the double-feature. Four hours of films, little more than re-runs of TV shows we flipped through on eight channels with a crunch-control—"Victory At Sea," and combat scenes expanded to the silver screen where Audie Murphy, Bob Mitchum, and John Wayne won WW II each weekend as shells sprayed sand or water 100 yards into the air above our heads and bullets ricocheted off the rocks. One star always took a shoulder wound, a half-dollar sized blot in black which didn't begin to keep him from waving his men forward toward the machine gun nest— hundreds dropping like flies as the cliché had it then. 10 or 11 years old, and any one of us, awakened from sleep, could say *Iwo Jima, Guadalcanal, Bombs Over Tokyo!*

Our numb young minds, our blind-folded souls never once asked, Whose idea was this? We'd learned it all by heart regardless of our sunny southern California life. Fair enough, our fathers said—we should not forget it was only 14 years since Truman dropped the A-bombs "ending hostilities." Thus as kids at summer camp we sang "from the halls of Montezuma" with no idea who Montezuma was, where his halls once were, or why marines were there in the first place.

We took it on faith, as we were trained to in Catholic School. And despite Holy Cards and the paintings of saints bleeding on church walls, the only thing we actually saw ascending was a mushroom cloud on the cover of *Life*, ash-colored of course, over some charcoal sticks— all that was left of Nagasaki. The Japanese—a people with whom we never should have had business dealings, a people for whom we had no remorse—had been BBQd, had gotten theirs.

So we had no real doubt about how the movies would come out, notwithstanding the Kamakazis and their suicide Zeros diving into the battle towers of aircraft carriers. We were safe, and could go to the beach the next day. This was our Saturday afternoon's entertainment, this was political instruction underwritten by Milk Duds or JuJy Fruits— all of it, we much later learned, orchestrated by FDR to pull us out of the Depression and put a chicken in each proverbial and impoverished pot.

High school soon enough, homework and the weekly quiz. We were 15 in 1963, and regardless of anything we learned in Mr. Kuehl's Modern History Class, we felt we were going to live forever. We parked our Chevys in the bowling alley lot across from school, turned up the radio re-verb and smoked rum-soaked Crooks or Hav-a-Tampas—little clouds of our indolence and unconcern drifting out the wind-wings into the amnesia of the sky. The cigars' wood tips tilted skyward in our teeth just like FDR's cigarette holder in that photo in our text, the one only a few pages over from the open graves—bones and skin white as newspaper, death's black print all over the bodies at Belsen and Birkenau.

We filled in the blanks, made our best guesses at multiple choice, but knew FDR, Churchill, and bloody Uncle Joe—how they'd hacked-up Europe between them like a shepherd's pie. Even further back, in Bible History, we'd read how Assyrians, Hitites and Chaldeans descended and took over on the plains, and about the failure at Thermopylae as well—they just kept changing the implements, the front men, the systems of delivery. And earlier that semester we stood and recited what we knew of Bosnia and Herzegovina, Gavrilo Princip and the Serbian Black Hand, the triple alliances that produced WW I with mustachioed archdukes in plumes and pointy hats. But we never heard word one about the industrialists and bankers that it fed, about the millions left in the French mud for nothing—their bones still coming to the surface in cabbage fields. Not a word against Franco who invited Hitler in to bomb the Basques for practice.

The old men behind the curtain cranking up the smoke and flames fully expected us to get used to it, to continue to contribute to the gross national product of war. In Dallas, they gave JFK a parade when he cut the military money back, and ordered the rest of us in our late teens to Indochina in support of General Dynamics, Colt Manufacturing, and Dutch Shell Oil, offering the Domino Theory and Gulf of Tonkin on the story-boards for *Face The Nation* and *Meet The Press*. Join up, leave, or enter a lottery for your life. So we rolled the bones against the *laissez faire* forces of our fate, and no matter what final grade we received, uniformly forgot Eisenhower's one worthwhile and departing sentence about the military industrial complex.

They counted out the body bags, counted us in the streets, counted on us to chip in for the peace and freedom of share holders and CEOs, who saved us the trouble of going to town for the double feature and newsreel, who brought it into our homes each evening, the news anchors reading the official tally and press releases of death. And though everything we'd learned seemed to relate, it didn't add up by this point—and a bunch of us flat out refused to pay the price, to sit there any longer in the dark.

Guardian Angel

...he may be that blue issuing from a tailpipe
of a car idling in the road.—*Gary Soto*

Out late, tooling-around in my father's sport's car, four wheels drifting
through the hairpin turn, snaking the S curves by the Bird Refuge, I
was lame-brained and lost it, came up sideways on a cement wall, one
with my name—*boboso, dick head, Joe Mama*—sprayed all over it. For a
second, I grew calm, almost resigned to my fate, then the sprung torque
of two revolutions bit, spun me back and flung me singing *Jesus Crippled
Christ!* across the two oncoming lanes toward that mud and shallow drink
where, stomping on the brakes, I stopped short with nothing more than
the black boulevard of night whizzing past my ears.

Lucky—in a way—no traffic or I'd have been grease, a glossy
smear for a quarter mile. But it had to be more than luck that lifted me
through the blind intersection at Indio Muerto and Voluntario where
Orsua, Desmond Olivera and I were T-boned by a cancer-infested late
'40s Merc doing 50 if it was doing 5. Airborne, kitty-corner, we mowed
down an oleander hedge and nailed a pepper tree before spinning out in
someone's front yard. Out of nowhere, two guys in black bowling shirts
looked in the window and said, "Futas! You crazy kids give us the booze
now before the cops get here."

We counted our ten fingers, looked in the mirror for our teeth. Who
was watching then, who knew we were coming and had been standing
unnoticed in the street lamp's violet arc, slowly cleaning his fingernails
of the past so there would be room for us to arrive unscathed and dazed?
Who put his hands over my eyes at impact as I lost count of those dark
seconds forever until I came to rest cattywampus on that lawn? How else
to explain— sober as scientists and climbing out the driver's side without
a scratch, all the parts in our Brylcreemed hair still in place?

How else could I have edged away from the dark licks of Death as
he rode next to me each day as I drove the foothills home—peeling a
tangerine with his teeth, his grey skin all but invisible as he squeaked across
the vinyl seat, rolling the wind wing out to spit and call up little swindles
of dust where my '59 Chevy Biscayne fish-tailed on retreads slick as seals

and its wide fins carved their initials in a sycamore before sending me and the whole two-toned caboose headlong toward an arroyo? Who was on the shoulder with his thumb out, whistling an old Perry Como tune as my axle snagged an oak sapling and yanked me to a stop—hubcaps flying off like lost galaxies, front tires spinning just over the edge of night?

Again, I walked away, but I didn't hear bodiless voices sing above me in a code known only to the dozing clouds and distant spheres. And though I paused staring up into the oil-blue vault, I knew I wouldn't see some chariot charge across the sky in an alphabet of flame or revelation, or even warning for the unconscious conduct and weak vessel of my blood. Wasn't I 17 and already living in paradise on the California coast, most all the documents of pain yet to be delivered or misfiled in a place as forlorn as Philadelphia? Wasn't this just the motoring life that had you slathering Bondo onto your lead-sled with numb enchantment, and, which at worst, left you wondering, whistling when you looked back? Yet I heard something snap, like a green branch where no one was, or if not that, a sound like tumblers clicking in a lock, a tiny brass weight plopped on the metal plate of a scale....

All this came rushing back as I was about to cross the swirl of headlights laser-beamed around Logan Circle—a humming hoop of light with cars switching lanes like electrons, where the civic fountain was fumbling a few coins of froth and I never should have been directing my attention the very moment a black sedan shot right by my shoes, a spot where I'd just jumped back, startled the instant before by honking and a bonfire of brake lights ascending the dull air not twenty yards away: some bum—not my father—but with the same galvanized hair fanned swan-like, TV evangelist-style, was almost clipped by an Infinity J-30, and despite curses and a chorus of horns, was holding his ground with a low, bending sweep of his arm, a less than sober version of a matador's best move. Then, running his hand through his hair like a symphony conductor, he threw his head back, looking skyward past the trees frozen there like cracks in the dome of dusk, and proceeded across the stream of lights as a gust caught the tails of his greasy raincoat, and set them flapping, like wings.

Ignis Fatuus

Swamp glow of the Milky Way. Bright platter of dust, arms coiled around the galactic hub like fiery streamers in a black wind…unaccountable, too many stars ever to be of use.

It's no longer enough to be allusive, like some minor movie star, collar of his black jacket turned up, smoking, overlooking the harbor lights in Denmark. That old film, that minor philosophy glinting off the waves….

Past 50, and death is no longer some distant city off in the analogical hills, a theorem you will never have to prove. The scientists have shown that everything returns to something—dust to…stardust, of course, so literal, cold, so removed.

Whatever it was I used to believe about reincarnation, I've lost hold of it now. And I remember I had some notion about art, how it might sustain a vague apotheosis beyond breath. Velazquez, for instance, stood there looking out from *Las Meniñas*, as if he knew. When he was made a Knight of the Court, that blood cross, that star on his tunic flaming over his heart, signified that he could move among glittering society. And his painting, well, a brilliant means, but not a self-sustaining end.

In his later years, my father believed he had been Velazquez, or possibly the king who hired him. He must have overlooked those portraits in the background—hazy, fading in the mirror as they would soon fade in life. And how, if he'd looked, could he have ignored Christ foreshortened by Mantegna—the grey sticks of the son of God's feet poking out the canvas at us? Or Caravaggio, his own head hung in the hand of David, offered to the dark—at 32, his tired, moon-dead eyes?

Pythagoras proclaimed everything could be solved by the arithmetic of stars, the universe just an algorithm of notes, chord of vibrating light, burnished to blood-dull. Babylonians cataloged 1,022 stars on a thin celestial globe, a surface which equaled the boundary of heaven— rotation of moon and stars the only dim points to show where they were heading on earth. The world barely spinning then….

Once I could have been found creek-side—bright mist burning at the edge of dawn—content tossing pebbles in a pool, all the time in the world in the relay of silver ripples…. But I never saw angels sauntering among the illuminated trees, no annotations in the paraffin sky. Just the wind dying in the oat straw, in the star thistle's purple heart, its starry spikes.

As close as I ever came was at 15, surfing Miramar Point. Salt water and blood rumbling with the breakers, crouched in a glassy tube, cutting back across the lip to stall and shoot through the curl again for the synergy of atoms and flying space. Which is surely the reason I was there, though then I didn't have the first idea…as I calmly released myself to the cold seconds burning by, to that point where I felt the electron click of green and yellow light at my fingertips flash out above the salt static and the froth, to burst clear, breathing where light was my immediate future, and not all that far removed.

Ars Vita

The last island and its inhabitant,
The two alike, distinguish blues,
Until the difference between air
And sea exists by grace alone,
In objects, as white this, white that.

—*Wallace Stevens* "Variations on a Summer Day"

Even on an island, anonymous as a wave—the Mediterranean and all this space and time shifting by—it's still the same sky at the window, hawk circling in the sun, same questions with their blanks waiting to be filled in. And there it is—just air. It only carries in your clouds from farther off, and the clouds puff up like, well, like clouds, but you can't let things go like that. No, this is serious business, putting your life piecemeal together. A few honed bones, whole cloth, and sweet sounds blossom from a pittospporum hedge just below the apparitional pines— and Jesus, you will not stop praising the birds. They too had somber beginnings, like the clouds, dark and in a minor key, that belly-crawled across Europe's old hills.

Now you prefer the more equatorial view—red macaw running on in the banana palm, a cigar-gold rum reverberating its major chords throughout both hemispheres of the brain, longitudes and meridian, the sun-rubbed demarcations between old and new dissolving from where you sit. But it's only the same sequence of neurons firing from bases of the double helix which brought us up from fish, and you feel free to fall back as far as you like to keep the grey globe spinning with sound and sight: "Moonlight Cocktails," "Old Buttermilk Sky."

Or you come up to speed with atoms, their geodesic domes collapsed and recycled from some star in Plank Time, a nanosecond into the big burn, atoms which now construct your heart, its unweary sea motion that floats the brain outward in a speculative atmosphere, surrounded by those very unastonished stars, or held off by a dusk leaving its high water marks across a lemon field thirty years ago—a little yellow smoke lifting to where the wind arrives unannounced, speaking to no one.

You asked for it, and so return to rifling pockets in your houndstooth coat for the scraps and sea-blue palimpsests. This is full-time, taking notes, all the reasonable alternatives exhausted long ago: shepherd, theoretical physicist, key grip, architect for the blind, action-hero. Nothing new there. So you figured you'd better mix it up, keep things moving, bring out the birds again, the pomegranates opening with their martyred light. Or perhaps something more *au courant*—the insomnia of waterfalls, the algorithmic rhapsodies of words alone, that relative cellular automata of language dissolving like comets in their bright ices and dust?

But they'll know it's you when the string section swells offstage and clouds slip into view in black & white gliding beneath the bare feet of some old saint, (a handful of Bernini sunbeams thrown in for special metaphysical effect.) The clouds of course were white, church bells rinsing out the March sky, cut out of sea-colored construction paper, the floating absences then held before your bleached home-room wall.

And here pigeons are homing above the sun-drunk roofs, wings brazed in unison, white again as native fishing skiffs also tethered on a line to the blue, as your boy's white heart kite-like over a field of alyssum on the way home from school—grey sweatshirt tied about your waist, sparrow in the guise of sparrows, you're barely above the level of the fence posts as dust settles down the west. You're fooling no one, and five will get you ten you're humming some sappy bars from "Moonglow" or "Theme from the Moulin Rouge," thinking you'll soon throw off awkwardness in favor of romantic sophistication as easily as Jimmy Dean flips a smoke into the street or runs a comb through his ducktail before he blasts off in a hot rod Dodge. Next party, you'll keep the calypso beat, dip and glide like Harry Belafonte as the '50s drift off like fog, like the little sleep and dream, which, at best, they were.

And what about all that air back there thick with a varnished light? No point in ignoring your life now and giving in to style. And fame? That pink fin-job flop-top Cadillac and its chrome roared down the highway to Boca Raton twenty years ago. Eduardo Pérez-Verdia knew, and he told me in 1962—being a Senior and therefore a man of the world—that the secret to success, especially as far as singing and Elvis Presley were concerned, was a sexy mumbling. And though the great poet has said, *Air is Air,* what is that to you? Corazon! Close the Cantina!

Send the men in pinstripes home. Get the movie stars out of the surf. Roll up your sleeves and praise the first thing that moves up there— what more is there finally to have at heart?

Twenty years—you keep shaking yourself, looking for the angel's bones, the latest lexicon of light. You sift the bromides and debris for that kid's lucky pocket piece, lost between the matinee and home as he flipped it into the winter sky above the shops—misplaced emblem of an unconscious belief in almost everything under the sun. Oh, it was only silver and worth a buck, but it had a bird whose wings—sometimes standing on a foothill stone—flew out of his ribs into the evening sky. I'd open both clenched fists and feathers would blow loose up in to the chorused clouds.

Nothing close to this, of course, took place, but to put it in perspective, I put in more than my fair share of time on top of boulders, longing and imagination working overtime as I addressed whatever was glowing in the live wires of my bones, pin-balling atom to atom to the west and back with no way out, no way to open my hands and lift off even a little at ground level, but there nonetheless.

It wasn't wisdom, for I'd regularly gone down in flames in Spelling and in Math; and it was nothing close to grace for I'd watched the girls, a sunflower haze all about them as they spelled everything and walked away in the white music of their blouses. But I could feel the voltage, those transactions in the blood which kept me floating over the waxed linoleum of a world where, despite low marks for comportment and penmanship, I loved almost everything.

It strung me up in the pear-colored afternoons, in the pepper scented mists of eucalyptus, and sang through me in a code sublime as the sea, and I feared next to nothing alone along the jetty at low tide or high in the avocado trees. Closing my eyes, my arms were full of birds, and facing into the wind I named the nine planets and nearest stars, called out five full Latin names for clouds. I was a force in that murmuring world, a source, as it turned out, unto myself. Yet I had nothing anyone was calling Promise—for instance, I made no more of rain than the next one in line as Monday poured down and the rooms went dim with breath. Nor did I sport what could be called Confidence as I set off on Saturdays in the neighborhood looking for friends with a hat and six gun, a silver star on my shirt showing, if nothing else, my allegiance to the skies.

Not long after this, the gentlemen in bow ties and tweeds lectured me about "disinterestedness" and "disassociation of sensibility"—something I was supposed to have or my writing wasn't? I was reading Swinburne for the grand rhythm of great angst and the emotional sea foam of the sound. I was told to absorb Dryden, and thereby, at 19, improve my style in prose. Bleeding Jesus, the paint came peeling off the walls, and the clear voices of my age went unheard as I sat in the campus grove closing my eyes between lines, coming back to the world and wondering what I'd missed—a good bit of everything going in a blur. Who were the Manicheans exactly? Were we or were we not in Cambodia, and what difference did it make to the Vietnamese and the forests we'd already fried? What could I possibly say about that when I was called on to stand and speak? It wouldn't help then to engage in yet another Liberal Arts discussion about what Aristotle considered to be truly "treeness"—although I still loved trees, and like Matisse, always wanted to keep the windows open to allow leaves and the calm labor of their light to sift in. Looking up, I wondered if perhaps trees weren't the last channels to heaven? Years later, drinking sherry in an off-season flat, I'd stare through pines to the sea or to the sea clouds and conclude that, Yes, that must be so—loosely anchored to the earth as we were by the fourth glass of fino, the hum and three-quarters glimmer of the soul circling the amber bay off Barcelona.

Perhaps I should give up on trees, embellished by clouds or plain against the air, palm fronds glinting with pewter as daylight glances down? But I can't abandon the old loves for even two lines. I'll admit I'll never make a comparison as surely as they breathe light, and may well not live as long, but against such odds as the dust builds up, I might as well do the little that I can—home or half the world away, content myself with the cloud-sweep over the umber hills, yucca blooms carrying their immaculate prayers to the sun. The short roots of my legs are trying to take hold—I shake a little in the winds, the tides of orange blossom, sage, and salt—I raise both hands to the light, surrender in my white shirt to the inescapable sky, breathe out, and say this.

After a Reading, Charles Bukowski Returns & Gives Me the Lowdown on Fame, Mutability, the Afterlife et al . . .

I'm not even drunk!—we both say that—as, ship-size and grey, he floats in…. I'm on the second floor overlooking the motel's postage stamp pool. The TV's turned itself off, and I've drifted in and out of the hot arms of a Santa Ana wind, door open to the background tracts of ocean and boulevard.

His face is still rough as a potato, and right off he tells me to open us a Bud, and light up one of those knock-off Hondurans—even the smoke and ash of this life are still beautiful, he says. Set that bottle over here by the window where I can remember it, you don't need another one—tomorrow, no one will care who didn't show up.

Hell, I'm gone five years and I'm still publishing more than you— the books just keep coming like horses rounding the turn at Santa Anita. Life's not fair—but death's no nap in the park. Listen pal, I had a huge backlog, one publisher, and no awards—I didn't gripe, and I never did drink as much as I used to.

You'd better just keep up with your typing—you're not young enough to complain anymore. The days run away like, well you should know that one at least—like taxis at rush hour in New York let's say, but I can't help you there. You've been out of the friends-and-glory loop since the get-go. You don't really want to be one of those three or four book Selected Poem types—then what's left? Look, there's nothing they haven't already not given you that they can't give you anymore—you're bullet proof. Have another on me, but spare me the rhymers and one more villanelle—Jesus, just remember who you are, those holes in your sneakers in grammar school, and write something someone will want to read before they die.

Besides, there's no one over here in a monkey suit passing around silver trays of sandwiches with the crusts cut off and a pitcher of Manhattans, little envelopes with awards from the Academy. Nothing really changes. Someone goes around with stardust and famous sport coats, all fitted out before you arrive. You have to be in line with the forty-dollar haircut and a handsome mug. Christ, you might even have to have a theory. It's tough all over.

All that stuff happens over a famous lunch—it's just the arithmetic of fate, like comets rolling up more ice and dust, or a sandwich wrapper on the sidewalk gathering more flies. Yeah, I read about that Prix de Rome, guys in pressed pants walking the Via del Corso praising the pines, memorizing names of Italian aperitifs when there's perfectly good beer—all on the government. It's nice work, but you're not in the club.

I voted for the Prix de L.A., a tab at The Pantry—a porter house steak and scalloped potatoes—but the phone never rang. Something like that Argentinean grocery in Glendale with the pungent sausage, spinach pie, a jolt of yerba maté. What you live for everyday. Stay home and work with that. Even a crude bastard like me still knows the real music of the world hanging above the avenues. Hell, I even loved German opera—any chump in a cheap restaurant knows Italian, but Jesus, that might be what love is? I know, I know, you think I should have a handle on that one by now, but I'm only dead, not enlightened.

As far as I can see, the freeways are well lit, and hazy or not, light is light and it falls gloriously every day somewhere in the world, like butter melting on rye toast—just don't flinch and praise some jerk's bad poems to get in one of those anthologies, or to catch a ride in his Lexus to some celebrity party at a swank place in the hills, and some of it will get to you. Cities of light, lots of light—everything radiant as hell. But where does that leave you?

If you're like me, it leaves you still dreaming about a small fishing village on the east side of Baja, a place where no one expected anything of you beyond a sloppy rendition of "Cielito Lindo" in the cantina on Saturday night—a place 20 years ago when even a measly royalty check bought you a thatched cabana and peace, shrimp the size of your fist, and the empty bay of Cortez was as far as rewards went on earth, each sunset the fish jumping blue and silver from the unappreciated beer-gold sea.

Home Alone In Black & White

Nothing on TV I haven't seen, so it's *Dodsworth* from 1936—self-made auto tycoon, slacks up to his armpits, a plutocrat, comfortable prosperity, propriety made for the movies. He sells up to the big concerns and heads to Europe with his money and his socialite wife for a grand tour, a second honeymoon. He's got to get over the idea that Americans can't quit until they die—sit under a linden tree, worry about how cold his beer is. He's going to see the world and get to know himself, and his wife—going to enjoy life if it kills him.

She is desperate to escape the Midwest, the Garden Club, and get on the boat, wants to dance, still has her looks—30, 35? And how elegant everyone on the ocean liner is. David Niven so young, his wire-thin mustache and hair slicked back with Brilliantine. Right off, he's romancing Dodsworth's wife, and she's happy to show her goods while Dodsworth's wowed by the geography and light on the coast. She is worried about her hair, and is wearing a luminous champagne-colored cocktail dress as they come into England. He wants a drink brought out on deck where he is looking at Bishop's Light, Jane Austen comes to mind. He says when he's old enough to know what he's after, he's going to…though these '30s actors are always older than I am from where I sit in the black & white worm hole of my living room 71 years later.

"Bishop's Light?—Look at my hair!" she says as Niven pours a nightcap, and the sea sails by out the window of the suite…. Nothing's explicit, but you know Dodsworth's not minding the store, and Niven is helping himself. No, Dodsworth's taking in the world, or the Italian coast at least, taking the launch into town, walking around admiring things until he meets up with Mary Astor, a widow, aging, but still a dish. And Dodsworth is not a complete fool, and gets the picture of the goings-on, his wife so self-absorbed and dismissive. He lets her go and takes up platonically with the widow, goes fishing in the bay, loosens up, gets a life, gets happy in late middle-age, doesn't let himself get lured back in, doesn't give in to guilt when his wife changes her mind as she sees the money-boat set sail….

I'm past it. I just hope my cats, who love me without qualification, keep living. I hate sentimentality, it takes the edge off most plots. But this evening, I have little choice. I'm marginally content with a glass of average chardonnay, a hint of ripe pears and butter, for which I did not pay $9.16 a glass—and half-empty at that—at the hotel by the beach in Santa Barbara, where a lot of Dodsworth's and their wives vacation these days.

Where there was no hotel in 1964, my last year of black & white, Alan Bates looking like a young insurance salesman in *Zorba*, and me in my senior year looking much the same—dark hair, thick and trimmed, out with my girl friend, probably our last movie together, which means our last anything as that is all there was going then. I wasn't wise enough at 17 to want to be Anthony Quinn, who as Zorba daily rolled the dice and accepted what came up, who took off after his life on a donkey or a boat, embracing whatever he could get his arms around....

And Jesus, if I fell down and hit my head, or went to sleep and woke up with the orchestra coming in and the grey clouds drawing themselves apart and the old prop planes and the parochial melodrama of the air, I'd be happy to go on walking into a dream on the Mediterranean coast or the Montecito shore—much the same, thank you—thank my lucky stars.... I'd be there *In The Good Old Summer Time*, with somebody playing *The Blue Danube*, walking beneath the sky thinking *Somebody Up There Likes Me*, and I'd have it all without throwing a single punch.

The Sea Again

The sky is anchored to your feet, the stands of eucalyptus moored against midnight; it doesn't look like anyone is going anywhere. Wake me in the dead of night, before I can clear my head of the dark swells, and ask me what I truly need. I will answer, *A handful of birds*, or, *God Made Me*—both are true. Western bluebird, sunset red breast, my arms empty but for the equivocating fabric of the air, the old notes always up there above us. We filter the present through our memories of the past, and, strictly speaking, we live there. Our brains take time to process what we think—the present happened some time ago.

Rote memory and the feedback loops to the pig-iron sentences in the Baltimore Catechism: Who Made You? Why Did He Make You? And I sang back the answers, but what I knew in my breath and in my blood was *Kickball, Thistle, Oak Tree, Wave*, and, as God himself would not appear, I accepted substitutions in the sky, and took in equal parts of oxygen and doubt.

Whatever the oceans once dreamed washes away or is flayed in the caucus of smog. The fish can't breathe. No architecture of light, no revisionist history is going to change the now and the then. Nevertheless, my 56th winter, and any day is a good one.

If the soul has a window, it looks out on spindrift, salt, our little life aimless as the old ostentation of the stars—the earth imperfect, eternal—the red planets and spiral galaxies rising up like orange peels on a dark tide. I don't care, finally, if God is terrible, or vengeful, an old God. Let there be something sturdier than the sea of grasses, the diminished plains. Some days I think the waters turn white with His worry, some days with the torments we've invented. Who could blame Him, if He's grown disinterested, if He's given up? No matter what I think, I just hope there is some there, there—beyond the clouds, the waves, the shadows on the empty surface of the sea.

Doing the Math

Young, I said, Bet high and sleep in the streets. Four-the-hard-way. Eight, skate, no rotate. Read 'em and weep! For style, I had my dead step-father's cashmere sport coat, a black-and-white herring-bone with three moth holes in the left cuff, the inner pockets stuffed with notes, with lines, I was convinced, of inestimable value. I was pushing ahead arrayed in my shoulder-length hair. I wasn't adding the numbers up— biological, chronological, or ontological. I was writing free verse. Who cared about the odds?

Now, there's not a chance in hell I'll find myself down on my knees, back in the kitchen of Jimmy's Oriental Gardens, rolling the bones with fate and the fry cooks against the greasy brick, salt from the sea breeze kissing my cheek for luck, luck that never made it through the screened back door. I will abandon hope and keep my shirt, and, given all I've laid down on ambition, come out at the same place in the road anyway, dust still spinning in the air from the last bus by.

These days, I consult the half dozen weed-thin eucalyptus, the two royal palms to their right, for a read on the sky. Gladiolas, the color of a deep bruise, have ascended to the level of the eaves, and are one more reminder about pride as the blossoms dry out from the ground up, before they fall…. After all the afternoons what do I have left? And though math was my weakest subject in school, the arithmetic of the wind is simple—plus or minus for a moment, everything blowing away through the blue leaves in the end.

With inflation and the price of bottled water, each of us is worth $23.99 in chemicals now, up from 87¢ in the '60s. I have graduate degrees in vagary; I've authored a monograph on the proper appreciation of spindrift, and have diversified my metaphysical portfolio. I've been wondering how many of Aristotle's atoms I've actually breathed in, how many I need for the full cathartic effect? The hot Spanish red of the pomegranate flowers, out in profusion, will, by October, deliver enough of the philosopher's fruit to weigh boughs down to the ground, as if they were pressing their ears to the earth to hear the arrival of some final accounting.

Middle 50s, and I catch myself hedging my bets, saying, See what the boys in the back room will have, each time I face the problem of the long division of the blue. Procrastination has slowly become a problem over time. I suppose the days stack up somewhere when they are done with us—like plates, rings, dark invisible chips. More and more I try to follow the example of my cats who stretch out on the chaise longue or in the high grasses of the un-mowed lawn, and I try to be instructed by them, who are not, in the fullness of their days, calculating anything.

Equally, I am trying to abandon a sense of duty. The leaves have a language beyond configuration. I have a sunflower and a pot of golden ranunculus, self-contained as light. I have thirteen rose bushes and never have been superstitious about splendor. Two volunteer blackberry vines, and my first bowl this week, crushed in the formula of sweetness on my tongue. Soon, I will go with my backpack to the mission, and steal a few handfuls of figs when no one is looking except God—as if he cared—and even if he did, by the time he chooses to manifest the square root of his will in the world, all our atoms will have likely re-combined into the untold statistics of the stars. There will be no one to give a fig.

Our unsanctified bodies, long past their sell-by dates, will flake away like chalk across the blackboard, working through their numerators or denominators, accounts overdue—dry as the dozen magnolia leaves scuttling across the patio like crabs. I have five fountain pens; I bring them to the table with my glasses and yellow pads, my hope for clarity and a small extravagance, the intemperance of setting down the sum total of everything I would praise or curse and only fractionally understand.

After three years, our lilac, just across the fence from our neighbor's orange trees, has produced one blossom whose fragrance would have multiplied the scented air of Babylon. The accumulated prayers from then till now equal an unrealized quotient. You can solve for X. Nothing carried over. With the heart's disposable income, you can invest in the ranks of gods or angels. No compensation, no guarantees. I am waiting for the cape honeysuckle and the honey-scented pittosporum to arrive on the evening air with the exponent of my soul, the nonlinear differential equation that is the result of the sky divided by the sea—my soul as transparent as the air. No remainder.

II

Conspiracy Theory: Low Carb Diet Conversion

Sweet Jesus, there's no way. I'm living it up with a Ry Krisp Light, an edge of Parmesan, a 6 oz glass of wine. It's the crackers levitating my cells and shouting Hallelujah. These days, it's all fishes, no loaves—not now, not ever again. These holey biscuits (and only a few) are all that are given unto me.

I've dropped 40 lbs.—another boat-load to go. Another platter of lettuce with vinegar on the side. I can eat eggs and all the animals I can get my hands on, my cholesterol shooting up like Southern California real estate prices. What I wouldn't give to be as emaciated as a saint, born-lucky, thin-boned, biologically redeemed from the get-go.

I'm trying to keep the gears and gizmos in the ticker ticking without electrical hiccups, without the ventricle bulking up like Schwartzenegger's biceps in his robot movies, and one day locking up in what my cardiologist mechanically refers to as Sudden Death.

"This Is Your Life," as Ralph Edwards said in the '50s on TV—it's black and white. He's long gone to his reward, but if he's lucky, they're not eating skinless chicken breasts and broccoli 7 nights a week in the afterlife. In any case, I'm not ready to look back from wherever it is there you get good reception.

For all I know, the soul in its grey shirttails and gamma rays circles the sky over a car-wash in Beirut, making amends for the shortcomings of the past. Hell, it might hover anywhere in the Middle East where there are no bombs or land mines, where even the poor—which is most everybody—sit down to stuffed grape leaves, hummus, babaganush, and celestial loaves of pita bread, steam rising like prayer without anyone giving the first thought to arteriosclerosis. If I found a family well enough off I could partake of a lamb's grilled leg, some cucumber sauce, a glass of cloud juice, and a bitter herb or two, but that's the limit.

In Iraq, armored personnel carriers and GIs sweep through the streets, handing out MREs and Hershey bars to kids as if WW II never ended, as if Vietnam's weekly TV slot had not been finally cancelled—bodies still stacking up like leaking sacks of rice. It's the same ball game, they just keep changing the pitchers. And given the pastime of organized national aggression, everyone's blood pressure is climbing like gasoline prices, and not just from the usual stress at the job, or the salt on the fries with that Whopper I'm not having for lunch.

Half the poor souls in the desert would praise the Lord for a box of Ry Krisp. But I'm bitter and disillusioned reading the labels—99 out of 100 companies adding sugar to everything—peas, carrots, tomatoes, even asparagus for Christ's sake—or not—and charging more. I should have bought stock in the omniscient high fructose corn syrup conglomerates, the ones with Dick Cheney on their Board of Directors. Sugar in breads, in fruit juice, in cereal, protein bars, processed lunch meats—you name it—none of which, for all my sins, I'm ever going to enjoy again. My bowl is filled with hard green pepper, celery, miserable arugula, soggy soy sprouts, and a slice of unmarinated muscle. And though it's written in the wisdom of the fathers that all things are possible, there seems precious little of that on the menu these days. Look around and it's easy to see that someone's always getting fat killing off the rest of us.

Time in the World

Last months of graduate school, and without the money to get out on the course, I took to hitting sand wedges over the house my pal Jon and I had rented for the year. I'd float a feathery flop shot from the front yard, above the roof and into the back yard where Jon would await the ball, then pitch it back to me. It was a sun-bleached pink stucco two bedroom tract house built just after the war, shifting toward chalk and dust, but as students we thought it fairly grand. It had a stove and fridge, and with a few aluminum lawn chairs, mattresses, a brown Salvation Army couch, make-shift desks and the usual cinderblock and boards bookshelves, what more could we expect?

The only custom feature of the place was a huge arched window in the front running from the peak of the roof down to the slab—maybe 8 x 12 feet worth of glass—staring me not quite squarely in the face each time I opened the face of the club and hit down, into the back of the golf ball with enough force to lift it softly over the grey gravel roof. If I'd thought about it, worried and lost even a little concentration, I could have easily chili-dipped the club edge into a clump of turf, bladed one of a couple dozen shots and shattered more glass than my meager grant, loans, and tutorial wages could repay in a year. But I could do this—no sweat—again and again given my gifts, my hand-eye coordination blessing my blood and nervous system, my unconscious deathless consciousness….

I never shanked a shot, and it never occurred to me that I had no business putting everything, the next to nothing I had, at risk. I never took a divot from the lawn, never pushed or pulled the shot to bruise the backyard aloe vera, never shook the plum blossoms from their branches along the fence, never hit one over those quarter-acre lots setting a starburst in the neighbor's sliding glass doors, never even knocked a knot out of the rain-softened fence. For no reason beyond the light singing all around me that spring, I was all confidence beneath the sky and green suburban leaves.

Jon had a 12 inch black and white TV, and, finished with our golf, we watched "Name That Tune" for laughs and the absurdity of the hosts, skipping the absurdity of the Nightly News. We'd have a glass of Jack Daniels while that bottle lasted, and then sit out as the stars swung around, listening for the music of the spheres. Jon had food stamps, and there was a butcher nearby who would give us a whole chicken, take the stamps and give us change. We threw every bit of every chicken on the hibachi, praising the intermittent bounty of our lives.

Classes and theses essentially done, the miserable workshop and theory-heads done, our reward was the calm evening, a little thoughtless recreation never worrying about what might happen, what might turn out wrong, or for the best. I kept my head down all the way through that fluid motion of my youth, and then looked up to see the small white dot moving against the blue, a stray fair weather cloud or two at the side of that wide fairway hanging there as delicately as the blossoms on the plum which our careless pastime never disturbed—the ball floating up there, almost suspended, while it seemed we had all the time in the world....

Productivity

First day of summer and I'm ground down, beat by another academic year, ego and administrative agenda, sea-weight of political grit—the mud pits, and the memo to make more bricks without straw…. I have no idea what it was I used to think about as I stretch out on the sofa, switching between baseball and golf on TV, the unguent expanses of green soothing my pan-fried sensibilities. I'm nodding out in the breeze from a new rotating Wal★Mart fan; like half of everything, it's most likely made by kids in China working 12 hour shifts, 7 days a week for next to nothing. I'm watching the dust of afternoon sift out the window screens. I'm only feeling a little guilt.

At least I'm getting some exercise, pushing myself up off the couch and walking to the kitchen for a non-alcoholic beer, then out to the front during commercials to check on my great grey cat, Cecil B. The June marine layer—equally great and pearl grey—is lifting, and the sun's bearing down on the orange and magnolia leaves, and Cecil's inspecting his weeds, marking the Mexican sage and broom, patrolling the invisible edges of his territory, ready for a good punch-up before the serious business of settling down in the shade of the Madeira bush for a nap. Cecil would not last a minute in a committee meeting, one of the many qualities I admire in him.

I should be useful, should be pruning the olive tree, the ceanothus bushes; I should be trimming limbs of the ornamental plum away from the phone lines, but with any luck no one's going to call. At my age, I have to be careful—skin cancer, sun stroke, dehydration—so I don my five-dollar straw hat, designed in Australia but pumped out again in China. I do a few minutes of watering, I drink another O'Doul's. I change the water in the cats' bowl, sweep the kitchen floor, but there is so much rust—legs, lower back, all the synapses creaking. I'm not fooling anyone. I need the true psychic lubrication of a Corona or Dos Equis, some time on the beatific beach in those ads, some flat-out rest like Cecil gets on his back in the patio shade, all four legs reaching unconsciously for the sky.

Back on the couch, the Dodgers keep fouling them off. I forget the count, and start to think of the jackpot of lingo right in front of my heavy eyes: line drive in the gap, nubber up along the line, a can of corn, pop up in an elevator shaft; he's on his horse, makes a basket catch, turns the twin killing, steps in the bucket, gets a piece of it to stay alive; boy can he bring it, pick it, dig it out, locate the split finger, the slider, the knuckle-curve; he paints the corners, goes up the ladder; someone goes yard, hits a grand salami, gets a bleeder to right; there are runners at the corners, he's stealing signs, he brushes him off, is run down in a pickle, hits a one-hopper back to the box, goes after the high cheese, gets caught looking; there's the squeeze play, the hit and run, a little chin music, and the jelly leg. I start to work up a title for a research topic, a grant proposal—I can't help myself—when I remember I think I promised a critical piece to some journal—a nagging voice for which I cannot find a mute button on the remote. What I really should be doing is rounding up all the fragments and unstrung phrases I've been saving on napkins, receipts, slips of paper—assessing the popular possibilities for the villanelle, a novella in verse.

These days I'm only drinking decaf and could really use a jolt of something chemically inspirational if I'm going to get beyond the dog-legs, duck-hooks, double breaks, bad lies, chili-dips, slices, shanks, blades, and fades. Mohandas Gandhi said that what you do will not be important but it is very important that you do it. I guess he was including me in that. I'm guessing he knew something about what was important. He had a wealth of good things to say—made a nation, got everyone to spin their own cloth, collect their own salt, take their turns raking the latrines–he wouldn't have survived in academia either.

My grandfather in the '40s, in Kentucky, was a big fan of Gandhi, far ahead of his time and place, especially for a farmer and county judge. And he loved baseball as well—my grandfather, not Gandhi. By the time I came along, he was retired under the shade trees, admiring the evening breeze moving randomly through the fields of timothy. He'd hire help for the harvest so he had time to give advice to men who drove up the long gravel drive and parked by the side of the barn and disused cattle pen, chewed and spit and discussed local law, the politics of the small river town he'd run for years. But mostly what I remember learning from him is how to take a pocket knife and whittle a stick down to nothing, casually, over an hour or two, and how it could calm you, and when to turn the portable radio on so we could lean back in the old wooden lawn chairs and listen to the Reds, live peacefully all summer with Kool Aid or sugary iced tea while Frank Robinson hit 'em out and Vada Pinson ran down the first base line like nobody's business….

The Semiotics of Ham & Cheese

For Dr. L.L. Zamenhoff

A tramp one morning on the road—a man who'd been living in a car, or
under one—all grease and rags, the mad strings of his bones stuttering
toward town…. I passed him near the convenience store, once more at
the entrance to a private drive near the courts, head bowed, a caked mop
of hair. Chanting to himself, he was bobbing up and down to ward off, no
doubt, the curious and civic-minded so he could rest beneath an elm.

A third time on my way from tennis before I stopped and walked up
with my ham and cheese, carton of milk—"You're a man who looks like
he could use some lunch." was all I managed to say, and without a word,
he unwrapped the sandwich and ate. What discourse then should have
passed between us fully signifying the new history of our social positions
on the earth? The meager bone-meaning was the oldest, the sharing of
food. His immediate agenda was hunger—mine, the unvarnished truth
of sandwiches and bare-faced need.

Who among us—standing here in his original skin—wouldn't say
he or she is deserving of the fruits and bounty of the earth, regardless of
the architectures of class, the encoded fallout of our various unspoken
privileges?

So, what—as my mother often asked—do I have to say for myself?
I feel impoverished for even telling this—for I did little to remedy the
anarchy of need with the impermanence of cold cuts on wheat. I have
not enunciated to any lasting effect, language that would move others,
let alone myself, to greater action—but then, at that moment, nothing I
could have said would have made more sense.

This morning, even the birds I count on to proclaim the sun's
beneficence, to expiate in their treatises, the self-evident ideals of the
past, are off somewhere more fashionable and bright. The wind goes
door to door and it doesn't take much to know that the silence it meets
with is all that's usually offered, all that could be waiting most any day,
for any of us.

We're still trying to unlock Etruscan, the obscure syntax of Etruria.
They left mummies, statues disclosing nothing in their inward smiles.
They lived apparently in harmony in their high, shining republics of

stone, developed sewer systems, civic rule, and more or less left the early Romans to conjugate and decline among themselves to the south.

What is there to say we're any closer now to diagramming the subject and object of the void? Hale-Bopp stops by every 10,000 years, a declassified composition of angels' wings and ice, a slowed articulation of white and whirling time. Every so often a falling star footnotes the dark coming for us all, glosses the dead air, without so much as a tinkling of glass or wind mumbling through eucalyptus. What new phrasing, what all purpose modifiers chorused against the night are we left with—what might sustain us, what language can we finally aspire to beyond the cold Esperanto of the stars?

The Assoc. Professor Crashes the Awards Program at The National Arts Club

Just like you, I wanted things—I was even prepared to wait. And so I volunteered for the Committee on Committees at East Jesus State, drove vans full of the semi-famous from the airport to the Conference on End Rhymes—at the Keynote banquette, ate the vulcanized chicken plate. I read from work in progress at the Alumni Christmas Fest, at the Fund Raiser for the Cryogenics Lab to an audience of administrators and pioneering subjects in the field…and came away with only psychic arteriosclerosis, additions to my list of colleagues for the hotel fire's top floor.

I never attended New York City soirees, or received a note from Richard Howard asking me around for Manhattans with some people he thought I'd find interesting to meet. And the red leather chair at the midtown club, the deferential man with a tray of little things on toast, the cocktail onions for my Gibson floating there like pearls, like the images for which I will never be known—they were tabled for a later date.

It's like looking over the shoulder of Scott Fitzgerald as he fox-trotted with the rich in his haircut and two-toned shoes. We've all seen the photos—the usual schmoozers congratulating this year's winners who took the train in from Princeton, again, or who simply caught a mid-town cab—the venerable Bulgarian formalist just discovered by the Academy, the influential publisher who writes pantoums.

I haven't even read in Minnesota, and now my honorarium wouldn't cover the rent-a-car. I kept my hand raised, applied yearly to the foundations (the phone never rings, and it's them) while the one-book-wonders scooped up the loot and lunched on the terrace at Bellagio discussing the merits of *terza rima* and plasma TV.

I've given up on living now even a little while in France, that apartment with charming neighbors calling over the fire escape, *"Guillaume, café au lait!"* I've despaired about Rome as well, the prize that would have had me, after lunch and a few aperitifs, walking under Respighi's pines. I even had my blue blazer cleaned and applied for a leave to write a monograph on the guards in Shakespeare's tragedies, their linguistic marginalization by privileged instruments of the state. I abandoned the one agent I might have had in the no-host bar, throwing back single malts on his Master Card and talking Oprah.

I was polite—it got me as far as Pennsylvania, and nowhere, fast. And so I take advantage of more immediate rewards, stuffing my pockets with cocktail sandwiches and fried wonton so I might regale myself later in the park amid the approbation of pigeons, the choruses of traffic as I toss the confetti of another ms. into the dark to flutter momentarily like the scornful stars. I'm no Delmore Schwartz but can play that part....

But first, before the spotlights and speeches, before the envelopes and insider trading, before the cameras flash and the critic lectures us again on "Language," before the Congressional poet recites from memory through his sententious teeth—I'll snatch another glass of up-state champagne from a tray, a sugar cube from the coffee service, and from my vest a shot of bitters, to help it all go down.

The Ponies on Chincoteague

They swam in on the waves—a Spanish boat breaking up offshore—and must have known anguish in those winters and the first bitter springs, the salt-wind freeze-dried and stinging their skins. But over time, they grew heavy coats and found every path to sweet water and grass, to the windbreaks on the inland side, the shaded marshes—the sky of their calm minds unconstrained among the arthritic trees, the holy shapes taken from wind.

Miles from the interstate, running the green range of this island barring the sea, I am not going to tell you that now they know no grief, for someone with rope and a shiny pick-up, with a permit from the usual official, has penned a group in a metal, make-shift corral, in a small open place where the sun steams through—to sell them, like everything else in America....

Sauntering through pine flats, along the sea flanking them on all sides, they were content with their own company, and never wondered about us, or the dust of clustered stars which must have seemed no more than marsh flowers on the bay.

In early March, ice still claiming the trees, you can beat the tourists and hotel rates and wander bundled up on the dirt roads or beach where you are recognized all day by no one but the gulls and half regretful motion of the tide. You can trace tracks down to the shore and just about catch a vague swishing of tails on the evening mist, a swirl of hooves flying toward the deepening blue. You can almost forget yourself in the resin-and-salt-charged air at your cheeks, discover that, for no reason you know, you're happy, running for all you're worth, back, on the last swell of light.

Patriot Act

Last Fall some worthless SOB bought the house in back and did not move in, but first thing cut down the healthy, full-lunged magnolia at one corner of the yard, then the fruiting mulberry at the other. My wife—who is not from here—confronted him with his electric saw in hand, balanced on a limb: "Why is it you Americans are always cutting down trees?" To which he replied that he wasn't, American that is, as leaves and branches fell until only a bare pole poked above the fence, insulting the sky. The mulberry disappeared, exposing TV and phone cables, the orange tree went un-watered until it was just bits of parchment on sticks. He couldn't be bothered to rake a few leaves and so scalped the skyline for a little expediency.

He demolished a housing complex for humming birds who'd spun their thumb-sized nests in the magnolia for years. On the central California coast there's not much winter, no reason then for the hummers to move south, yet they were gone despite our red feeder of free sugar juice suspended from the eave.

Now in April, the purple spiky plumes of the madeira abound, and three or four birds have returned nipping nectar, strafing my quick but resourceless cat, my long-suffering boy, back three times from the vet's for wounds defending his yard from interlopers who sneak into the neighborhood to terrorize locals. For five days I strung chicken wire over barb-arms atop my cedar fence to keep them out, and Cecil B. in. He has no freedom now beyond his yard, and need no longer defend a homeland one house either side of ours.

Late afternoon, I sit out reading and Cecil has his nap on the lounger. The hummingbirds come calmly to rest—two grey, one metallic green, and one ruby-throated—all on the top taut security wire, letting their frantic wing muscles relax a moment from territorial dog-fighting as they inspect their old lot of flowers and assorted shrubbery before needle-nosing the madeira spikes and Maraschino blooms of Mexican sage. And while the absentee landlord's lawn erupts with gopher holes—gophers Cecil used to police-up *nobles oblige*—the birds relax atop my chickenwire compound, sing and clatter, acknowledging a safety level they can abide, a loyalty to the blooming and uncertain world—as much theirs as anyone's.

Paris Dispatch

Oh lucky lucky life. Lucky life.

—Gerald Stern

I love a place as obvious as Paris. I'm staying at The Grand Hotel Jeanne D'Arc for $60 a night and I know *fin de siecle* bistros with *service compris*. I have an L.L. Bean cotton sport coat the color of the leaves along the *Champs Elysees*. I'm a beige tourist like the rest, and blend in along the river walk. I'm quiet and polite with my 75 words, and everyone still in town in August is nice to me when I say *Merci Madame* the way I was taught in kindergarten from our French nuns, Madame Rose and Madame Adrian.

I love saying *Boulevard Montparnasse, rue Monge, rue du Faubourg St-Denis,* and knowing the immediate, vibrant ligatures of the air. 4 years old and I pronounced perfectly phrases *en Français*, was awarded gold and silver stars on my school collar. Who else but the French can pile up so many vowels, such sonorous diphthongs over coffee with milk, offer the mellifluous directions of the boulevard, or the resplendent assonance of just ordering lunch?

Occasional clouds roll over the afternoon like *boules* the men are pitching in the parks, keeping the swelter down. Only an afterthought of rain around 5:00, just long enough to browse the only English bookstore and come out with the dust.

Almost 8 francs to a dollar and we are eating *chaume, morbier* and *reblochon*—we're drinking little cups of champagne at the neighborhood bar around the corner from our hotel. Our Metro stop is either St. Paul or Bastille—saints or revolution, this far over 40, it doesn't matter now. Still there's plenty to be said for doing nothing, for paying attention—anonymous beneath the clouds—to the aimless crunch of your shoes over centuries of decomposed granite in the *Tuileries*, over the bridge to *Ile St. Louis* or to the *Jardin des Plantes* where the dinosaurs have been up-dated and the flower beds appliqued with saffrons and blues, where the ancient pines and pin oaks loiter at the edges, just off *rue Lacepede* and *rue du Cardinal Lemoine*.

The first thing off the train in *Gare du Nord* I saw the sun-white domes of the *Sacre Coeur*, and took off down the wide sidewalks blessed with light, putting one happy foot in front of the other with that expansive feeling that you're going to live forever—and my mind flashed to the cover of *The Red Coal,* that black & white photo of Stern with Gilbert in 1950—thin and serious among all the Parisians on the generous pavement. Stern, too young, of course to know what he would understand 30 years later about Pound and Williams, about fame and obscurity, and knowing the one lesson time teaches you: to love obscurity, attached as it was then to the thin fellow and world-beater-to-be in baggy trousers. Now what wouldn't you give to be, as the old song has it, "young and foolish again…"?

And there we were, Veinberg and Santos and me 17 years ago, hoping someday we'd be somebody, thinking how lucky we were to be in Paris with enough in our pockets to survive the fall. I thought of little beyond the lovely trees, shopping at the *fromagerie*, buying lamb and *beaujolais nouveau*, returning our wine bottles to the little shop for 20 *centimes.*

17 years ago on these boulevards thinking about the great poets with Veinberg and Santos, knowing we weren't them, but that at least we had poetry pushing out the long phrases of our breath. On autumn mornings we walked down the promenade in the *Jardin des Plantes* between the barbered sycamores—happy in our old clothes after a night when we almost again did not drink too much after hours at the Dixie Melody, listening in that stone basement to someone as flawless and smoldering as Carmen McRae, and walking out of there to the early sun spiking the sleepless river….

Yesterday, I mailed them sentimental postcards of the autumn trees lining the Seine. I've been waiting 17 years to feel this way again. The pink neon still buzzes outside the Dixie Melody, the sidewalks wide and unending, and our lives, more or less, burning away imperceptibly like the little fragments of smoke from the chestnut vendor's coals. If we're lucky, we'll find ourselves on a street, stopping at a small table and happily ordering an over-priced coffee to watch the world go by a while, knowing there is nothing like it, nothing better, as long as we're here….

Time Change

for Larry Levis

Waking in the dark, daylight-savings gone, I'm remembering the Biltmore, killing the afternoon at the MLA in '81, the hopeful with their haircuts upstairs being grilled like fish. I knew better than hope. I'm remembering that dark bar Larry and I had all to ourselves, and a hard, green chablis from a jug at $3.19 a glass which unscrambled my nerves enough so I could ask about his work. And yes, I said "work," trying to sound as if I'd packed some scholarly resources in the inner pocket of my sport coat, trying to sound objective, although I had committed at least a hundred lines to heart. He looked up to the one blade of afternoon light slicing through a transom and said what he was trying to do was stop time, casually, the way he'd say "Fresno" when asked where he was from…and that, to me, rang as true as a tree, or a shoe, made sense as clearly as a star burning through to this one blue dot in the outer precincts of the Milky Way.

I was treading water there. 30, I think, orbiting out in the provinces of community colleges. What I understood about poetry would have fit on the back of a beer mat, space left over for a quote from Machado whom I had yet to read, who would later show me all that could be lost in a hive of clouds. Larry lit a Marlboro—we weren't going anywhere— and, as indifferently as he tossed a match into the ashtray, told me I was a "good poet," as if it were just a fact, something that kept me going for years.

Interviews ending, we met a friend and headed up the street despite the procession of tweed coats walking back saying the nearby *Ristorante* was booked. It was an old post office made swank with pastel couches and kidney shaped glass tables, a place I'd recognize twenty years later in a film. The maitre d' stopped us at the door for reservations—a friend of a guy who'd married one of Larry's sisters, who wasn't sure he remembered Larry, and asked about his father, not hearing he'd died. When Larry told him, he raised his hand and we had a table before we could see we were in over our heads. I ordered the ravioli and was told it was an appetizer, a few bits in a thin sauce at fourteen dollars, a lot of money then. We had a tiny veal chop, a bottle of the cheapest Montepulciano and pulled every dollar bill from our pockets to pay the check—that long ago, not one of us with a VISA card. 45¢ for a tip, we waved and stepped out quickly, still hungry, to the street, grinning with our impoverished luck.

What do we ever know? All I had, I thought, was time. 10 years since his heart stopped, and no simile for that. I have some letters, notes in the loop and ligatures of his hand. Phil has his Parker 51, Bruce says he still shows up in dreams. And even in Fresno now, everyone sits out at tables in the Tower District with over-priced coffees and cigarettes. Now, I can put everything on a credit card. The aroma of Parmigiano-Reggiano and Pecorino, logs of salami rising from Piemonte's Deli over Olive Street, anchoring me in the world.

Day after All Saints Day, I'm awake in the dark, thinking of Larry— irony moves right along…I'm too old to be a Romantic, too hard-boiled about the heart, but soft around the edges nonetheless. He'd shrug his shoulders and laugh to hear me advising my cats about the most prudent courses for their lives. Today, I halfway know who we were all that time ago at the Biltmore in L.A.—the miserable job conference where I did not even apply, where I went just to see people like Larry, to wear my one acceptable sport coat and blend in along the edges of those apparently on their way. I felt like a utility infielder lucky to be called up, briefly, as they say, "for a cup of coffee"—lucky to have an afternoon to sift through some of what I didn't know, lucky to spend a few hours with Larry who cared less for the posturing and unvarnished pretense of it all.

I'm still talking about dust—I can look back and see it swimming there where the sun cut in above the bar. Near the end, Larry was reading Coleridge's *Biographia Literaria*, wondering if our lives were enough, if they ever measured up? What would we change if we could? I can always single something out, but have little to complain about at this point—just time, and the variables of dust floating off toward the predictable dark. I'm here near the sea with all the air I can breathe. Almost 60, every long-lasting provocation of the spheres spinning above my head—and you, my friend, out there somewhere, still ahead of us in the light.

Dispatch from Santa Barbara, 2001

Mid-summer, July 4th in fact, but I'm not in town for the fireworks display from the breakwater. I'm here on errands, an emergency trip to the dentist, in and out before they crowd East Beach, Ledbetter, and the harbor, packing in on the sand thick as grunion under a phosphorescent moon.

I have an hour before I have to be somewhere, and I stop in Alameda Park where my mother first brought me as a child. There was a pool of shade under some trees and no swans drifting on a little lake, no roses, no hedges in the shape of a heart—precious little except the wood bandstand that even then was no longer in use. Little but that block of shade—Anacapa to Santa Barbara Street, Micheltorena to Sola—courtesy of Morten Bay Figs and Spanish palms, and the creamy, book-perfect, fair-weather clouds of the '50s going over the Figueroa range—since age 4, the clouds and trees carrying off my thoughts....

And today I think of Thomas Wolfe, the sad line anyone knows about home. He knew about time, the quick dusty path here below the clouds. Perhaps he knew what was coming with real estate on the California coast, way back when everyone lived in bungalows.... Now, making more money than I ever imagined, I am nonetheless dispossessed, can only afford to live an hour north in the wind and fog. I stand here, my feet on a sidewalk worn rough as beach sand, pavement I've walked off and on for 50 years, looking up to the blue or to the old clear stars, and it's hard to call it mine.

My work is 3 hours south of here, and so I'm driven in all senses, past what I love. This morning, I'm taking time off from the world to be in it, to turn back—in star time—an instant, to 50 years ago when my mother took me after a nap out to the free, green republic of the park, from our turquoise stucco apartment on Micheltorena. We had just moved here and no one had heard of Santa Barbara, no one cared it was here an hour-and-a-half above L.A., a sleeping arboretum even angels overlooked, where we had next to nothing, and everything, where father worked nights, and my mother and I ate fried bologna and tomato soup in the Formica kitchen in front of a GE plastic radio. I had this life beneath the cool plush oaks and I didn't know to ask for anything more.

The Bandstand still standing...the small metal harp at the top, the cupboards for dwarfs all around underneath...the criss-cross walk corner to corner, the honorary wino in his black thrift store suit and white tennis shoes, smoking alone by the chained-off steps leading to the platform where I raced around in circles when I was 4...the 2 obligatory people passed out on the grass, newspapers over their faces, the early silent heavy air going by, slowly it seems....

Beneath the star pines and magnolias, the voluminous pittosporum, the 1 jacaranda pushing out for sun, the 5 paltry redwoods, the single eugenia grown exponentially beyond hedge size, older than me...I'm counting trees, so I keep it this time. And I want to name the Joshua Tree thrown out thick and twisted, to appeal to Our Lady of Sorrows with its washed-out pink walls and bell tower across the way, as if this, or any of these lost listings could help me reclaim or hold my home.

This park, this place, as full and spare as I remember it at 4—no adornment but the leaves, the carved top of the picnic table, someone's initials sunk beneath the brown paint, from Catholic High up the street in 1954, the bare civic patches raked, and sprayed with a hose—part of the world that doesn't miss me, where, if I could, if I had more time, the simple wherewithal of dirt, I'd be here all my days, content as the trees for all the sky to see. As the acorn woodpecker laughing at god, and his good fortune, at the same sparrows and rogue pack of pigeons claiming the earth or whatever is left of it here alongside the 1 picnic table and the grass as they peck at the grains of light.... I join them again today, holding on to everything the wind has left to offer....

Spring Sabbatical

Wind-strewn, the thin afternoon clouds string together a rib cage, the white and almost transparent vertebrae of the blue. I don't know what the wind wants now, running its fingers through new leaves of pomegranate and podocarpus, buddleia and rock rose in my green and overgrown garden. What did it ever want?

Hummingbirds are at the cape honeysuckle and madeira—what do they ask for but the thrumming and varied appreciations of light? And me—now that I have a few minutes to stare off into nothing? Wasn't this my first occupation, one for which I showed exceptional promise, daydreaming happily in the grey classrooms of long division and fractions, handwriting exercise books? I was assessing the progress of March clouds as they inched through the butter-bright tops of the acacias just beyond the great framed windows, clouds whose sky-scrawl resembled mine with my Shaeffer cartridge fountain pen—swirls and blots above the sun-blistered sandstone peaks.

And if I had a soul—as they kept insisting that I did—with its parochial obligations, with its invisible tallies of plus and minus, then I understood it only there, just out the high transom, in terms of clouds where I was drifting along, breathing unconsciously with everything I would ever be worth, naming the lost continents of the chalk-white, midday moon.

What wouldn't I have given to recall that ten years ago before the petty academic scrapping got to me and threw off the rhythm in my heart like a scratch, a skip in an old LP? What would I give to fully know this, this afternoon lying back beneath the patio umbrella on my dandy plastic chaise lounge—the spring geraniums vibrant against the air with their lipstick reds and pinks, the marigolds in their pots brilliant as a ring of suns around the calm blue neck of that Hindu elephant god—something I would have easily believed back then.

The lawn already mowed and trimmed a week ago so I might come to this—30 minutes of decompressed mid-afternoon reflection, dozing with my great grey cat sharing the lounge, nothing to do but look around and exhale evenly through the almost empty sky, letting my blood download its indiscriminate freight, making some lighter sense of things, doing no more finally than it seems I ever should have in the first place.

CamphorTree

In memoriam: Ken Smith 1944-2007

Daily walk to the Post Office, around the neighborhood for my heart and general continuance. 2nd week of October, I set out with straw hat and stick, and though the rest of the New World is open for business, the Post Office is closed for Columbus Day. As I loop back, I come across a camphor tree on the corner still with its full complement of sea-green leaves—russet edged, heart-shaped bells holding on where others have started to turn in the unending on-shore breeze.

Yesterday, the message that you were gone, Sunday the 7th, and that you were not suffering now—which they always say—that you were no doubt arguing with someone about Plato on the other side—which they don't. They plugged a valve in your heart, good as new. But then the kidneys bailed, and hospital pneumonia closed the deal. I think you were just 64—in our 30s when we met. Whatever the math, you left a novel and a half, unpublished—told the administrators "I can only write them, not publish them."

Back in the dry counties of Kentucky, you helped me keep my head on straight amid a department of ill-willed country boys, until we both got out.

Driving cross-country this last time from the east, I found myself on the turnpike outside Paducah, approaching the Party-Mart where, the first of every month, we drove an hour each way to stock up on hard stuff and wine and haul back bottles for friends. Writing, the west, the hard work in bars, we talked the good people we knew, and always the last war. And so about the troopers at the county line—looking for bootleggers and boys smuggling booze—you were never concerned, having already served the worst sentence you could: "What can they do, give me helicopters and send me to Nam?" A mile from the off-ramp, it was all I could do to keep from breaking up behind the wheel remembering our trips in your green rust-bucket truck.

The breeze plays up, pushes my hat back off my head, the way a pal might, with the back of his hand, telling me to knock it off, cut the sentimental crap.

So I'll just say this. I hope the afterlife is not a decoy, something we've just made up to sit there peaceably holding our hopes. I'll say it in prose, meet you half way, hoping if there is another side of the river—though there'll be no need—we can have a drink, argue philosophy, or baseball, and I can tell you about that camphor tree, its simple glory, an extended brightness that we ran out of time to see....

Beginning With A Line from Tu Fu

Soon now, in the winter dawn, I will face my 59th year. I don't know that life goes anywhere, really, but thinking back on it in the moment it takes another leaf to fall, I can see how many more evenings I will need sitting out here—letting the wind pass calmly through my hands, overlooking the star pines, and jacarandas, the valley of home—to come to anything like a decision....

I think of Montecito, the friends of my youth, my home and the sea—green hills, that have traveled off without me now, despite the longstanding optimism in the stars.... I look at the brown haze drifting between here and the channel islands—I take an early drink, and praise whatever is left of my Fate—differing little, in all likelihood, from anyone else's....

I have no idea what I want now beyond everything I've ever had, all over again and the legs to withstand the long-term effects of gravity, continuing to have their way with me, pulling me back into myself like a disused star that will one day implode, invisibly compress beyond the heart, and somehow—the theory goes—withstand the heavens.

The wind comes from 10,000 miles away, the sweet air lifts the atoms of light. One thin cloud, shaped like a soul, is back-lit, briefly, by the moon. Whenever I can, I stare off into the blue as if something more than the resin of pines will linger on the air—the salt breeze rising over my head, the tracks of small shore birds unthreading back and forth before the tide....

III

Humility

Only 5 or 6, and I drove my father over the hill with questions. From the pressure beneath bottle caps to the space of space, I wanted the essential whys and wherefores, wanted explanations for the punch press starry nights, the invisible clockwork and counterweight of the moon, how the sea got in our blood in the first place—the physics of Physics outside the math I would never get. Where and why did space end, how was it we breathed air but couldn't fly? I wanted the Golden Book version of the Infinity Code, each molecule in the Big Bang alphabetized, the Tinker-Toy schematics for neutrinos, quarks, dark matter, and the postulation that would string several dimensions together for the Grand Unified Field Theory of Everything. You name it, Mr. Wizard, the wisdom at the end of wonder, presto-change-o—keep it simple and between the commercial breaks, and I'm your man.

Fifty years later, driving to the post office to mail out yet another rendition of my life, I wonder what I might ever accept without question? Why don't we just sit back for once and let mystery overtake us? Why not give in and let the stars scroll up without a spectrum analysis? I'm thinking summer evening fog, how I love it unfurling over the beach fires, mixing with the drift-wood smoke, tossing on my old fog-grey sweatshirt, even in July, and staring into the coals, into the last stars sparking out above the waves. The sea is faithful to salt, consistent with a certain dust and light across the prairies, but together with the stars, quantifies next to nothing on the long list of our desires. We're up against it here—the delirium of shadow and rust, the black and white reels projected on the cave wall, and the conundrum of the brain itself, electrostatic pattern-bursts, jelly jar that somehow holds and equals us, sea-thundered clips of fire from which we take any evidence of hope. No route for escape, just the incomprehensible all about us like clouds, and after all this arm wrestling with God, and no matter how many falls, who ever comes out ahead?

Under these grey stars, how do you keep the one-way stream of time from, by way of immediate example, dissembling your mother's life, your own? 83 years for her, whether or not you prayed or held onto your Holy Cards. Death is in those cards—we all took a hand—and it's 7-Card-Night-Time, every time. Maybe we need to keep our eyes closer to the ground? God's not sitting in the back room waiting for us to produce another theory. In their cellars, hermits praise the onion, some fennel root, and celebrate pitifully little beyond the redwoods that point away from the world. The glass-green sea of summer is the perfect backdrop for an ellipsis of lost wishes escaping like rain. We could blend in.

And this afternoon, if it came down to a choice, I'd take my cat over a Rockefeller Grant, I'm that ripe and soft around the edges now. Jesus, I feel something close to fulfillment just slogging through notes on a yellow pad, smoking a $2 Honduran *corona*.

I don't know anymore what I know beyond the gulls each morning singing the loneliness and the fullness of the sea, the old voice in the waves crashing on the rocks, recapitulating the empire and the ash of the heart. Whosoever takes nothing from the world was not here to begin with, or was looking the other way when longing was handed out across the sky. We may not need the equation for grandeur if we're the lucky 5% with the fruits of the earth and a weekend to worry about flower arrangements and recipes for shrimp cocktail. Who, finally, should we call in for questioning?

When was it ever difficult to want it all? Relative to God, the bald white moon has risen clearly above the afternoon, just over the blossoms of the neighbor's pear tree. We all have, it seems, some purpose, though vague, unfinished, undefined—all of us salvageable as sea foam from the sea....

Buckley y yo

Asi mi vida es una fuga y todo lo pierdo y todo es del olvido, o del otro,

—*Jorge Luis Borges,* "Borges y yo"

The other guy, the one working like a mule driver, he's the one picking up the crusts, saying he still knows someone in New York. I'm busy reading a little philosophy, dumbed-down books on astrophysics, though no one ever asks me what I know about gravity waves or the afterlife. Still, it's good, someone said, to be gainfully employed—no doubt one of those mule drivers....

But it's the other one and his sack of small potatoes who has me talking to myself—something's better than nothing one of us is always saying. Once, we let the leaves pile across the yellow lawn, living large, drinking jug wine, telling lies from the lawn chairs late at night, a few miserable legs and wings on the hibachi. Then, you finally get your nose above the water line and the skin and bones begin to let you down. You've got to wonder.

You and me, Borges and Santayana, at sea in a leaky metaphysical boat—if I'm the first one over the side, you're coming with me *hombre*, no joke. You sent the SASE in for the guidelines and got no reply. Poetry and philosophy will save themselves. So back to practical matters....

The tiny pebble that clicked against the office window. Did it fall from the beak of a bird, or was it taken up from an empty field by wind and dismissed by the blue? Did it travel millions of miles from the icy Kuiper Belt at the edge of the solar system just to get your attention for a second so you'd stop thinking about Time? Are we important enough for God to throw stones?

You still think there is a way to reason it out, to prove that you deserved better, deserve more? I went along, believed you knew what you were doing, but *viejo*, this far down the road chaos theory makes a lot of sense. Besides, there are more than enough pebbles to confuse us all, to fill the pockets of everyone who feels like walking into the sea. Not me. And I'm not about to drag you there either like a sack of stolen silverware.

Let's be realistic, throw our hands up and admit we're only ice and dust, some atoms fobbed off by an imploding star even God has forgotten, and despite what our boy Einstein said, just a cold roll of the interstellar dice, a happy coincidence when you consider that atoms are only 4% of the standard model of the universe. We're lucky there's so much as a harmonica wheezing against all that darkness, let alone our favorite, Gustav Holst, who wrote for orchestra, choir, opera, ballet, *and* the planets, excepting Pluto and Earth, where we stand at the shore of infinite waters, where Pluto has been cast back into the frozen junk pile circling in the dark. But what does cosmology have to do with book sales? Why don't you listen to your relatives and write a self-help Western, a home-improvement mystery? Strike "mystery"—you need to finish this before the next moon rises. You know what Pessoa said—"The only mystery is there being people who think about mystery." You buy that? Consider the Harris tweed in the Thrift that fit as if it were tailored for you, or me. That's 50 to 1 against intelligent design. Sure it's summer, but fog will soon be rolling in on your bit of coast, and then plenty of time to walk along the cliff wearing that coat and an old felt hat, recalling '50s black & white British films in which wandering about was a respected occupation. Again Pessoa—"To think of God is to disobey God." Does that clear the situation up?

We have a special relationship—we're never going to travel fast enough to slow down Time, nor that black well of energy pushing the planet out to the edges of who-knows-what, faster each year…. As the glittery facts play out, they're just metaphors for speculation—perhaps that is what's kept you going? But I doubt it. I see through you, *compadre*; you'd have written fewer of those homesick odes if something new was really up—you could never keep a secret. One glass of cabernet and you'd tell anyone where you hid the Krugerrands, if you had any.

If you go back and wander the streets and parks of your home town where nothing much has ever happened, you'll be perfectly content to let someone else try and work things out, explain the muddled dialogue between you and the eucalyptus, the molecular idiom, the one-sided explication of the clouds vis-à-vis your most recent image for the soul. And that young man interviewing you for a magazine, with questions about your early work, the theory behind all you've lost—you're doing a lot of tap-dancing to get around being just another Pozzo sitting by the sea. Jesus, did you ever think you'd have "early work"? I've done my share of waiting. I no longer dance. It's one thing to point to an influence, it's another to give the money back.

I'm happy a couple hundred people might see your work, but you're not trying to tell me any of it is unique before God, or even before the dead—a big percentage of whom constitute that 4% of everything there is in the universe?

We have our images of ourselves, like the full gold moon floating on the surface of the sea. So I'm the thin one with lots of hair, still hanging out at the beach in my 20s, blissful without a savings account or publications. You're still afraid to face me at the card table under the fig tree, the stars looking over your shoulder. Shuffle the deck and deal— 7-card no-peek-roll-your-own. Time and Eternity were concocted on earth. What more do you have to lose?

There is nothing up there our longing can grasp, even if I'm standing on your shoulders, or vice-versa. Why don't you copy out what ingredients we need for spaghetti arrabiata—you'll feel like someone just pronouncing it, yet that, no doubt, will remind you of String Theory again—who else might be, in some parallel universe, doing all the preparation so one of us can lean back and light up a *Partagas*, the smoke swirling off toward that asteroid belt.

Borges tells us his life was a fugue, but he wasn't talking song and dance, he meant that if there is something there—some conscious state beyond stars—what chance is there we'll remember who we were? Never mind about your notebooks and fountain pens, the transcendental trail of crumbs. Nothing comes up on Map Quest when you punch in "Oblivion." And if you're really so sure of yourself, why have you gone to so much trouble to write all this?

Philosophy 199/Modern Thought

What we can't say, we can't say, and we can't whistle it either.

—*Frank Ramsey*

Smartass 20-year-old, head-banging bored with Ayer and Wittgenstein, the few pages I'd read of Pierce's Pragmatic Theory. So didn't I shout, Sweet Jesus, it's all a bunch of horseshit on the wind! to my business major pals down the dorm-room halls? Young, Wittgenstein concluded that the belief language can capture reality was just bewitchment. Plato had, I guessed, handed off the ban-the-poets baton. Even so, I might have bought into his idea that philosophy is a therapeutic activity, intended to relieve the bafflement generated by misuses of ordinary language if only we'd got onto something besides toothaches!

Language/Philosophy—and then there was Reality? This was, after all, the '60s—Surrealistic Pillow, Purple Haze, Sgt. Pepper's, tie-dye, Tabasco Sauce, Haight Ashbury and Hare Krishna for Christ's sake. For weeks we were up to our eyeballs with whether or not we could know empirically if our tooth ached! I wanted to know who didn't know, and I didn't need linguistic goose-steps to prove the throbbing fact to anyone, let alone myself. I had passed economics, aced World Classics, and I didn't want to waste more hours each week in theoretical discussions, hours better spent bouncing on the bed, boilermaker in hand, Stones blasting on the Hi-Fi with the high and immediate message of hedonism.

And none of our instructors revealed that ten years after, Wittgenstein repudiated his earlier pronouncements, damaging the industry somewhat. I was a young man then, but quickly aging in that class. I was writing poetry—inward, sentimental, and so contorted that it took me only 5 years to repudiate it and burn the lot.

The Christian Brother teaching us had for years been known as "Clouds" due to his infrequent contact with the solid earth and thus any useful information you could carry away from the class. In our sophomore year, Socrates drank the Sparkling Hemlock for no reason beyond some language he'd espoused in a committee meeting, long before, it seems, the lyceums had councilors or ombudsmen, or the teachers had unions. Somehow, Socrates doing himself in over a few sentences never carried over to Wittgenstein and company and the toothache seminars?

Scratch my surface then and I would have jumped at any spur of transcendental knowledge, would have contributed at length to a discussion of the light around the tops of trees, had it—the question of that light—ever come up. Sitting by the window, I was an A+ day-dreamer and figured there must be something in back of the air? But no. Nothing like that was ever put on the table. Then in the spring, the adjunct Professor from Berkeley began the class with an Aristotelian inquiry into "Tree-ness"—the difference between the table, our desks, and the trunk of the acacia outside. The pain was palpable as rain, brain fog flooded the room. Even the numb-nuts who'd had a tracheotomy as a result of chugging a pint of Seagram's 7 could work out the compare-and-contrast on this one—no syllogisms, no purple cows required. We'd read Euripides and Aeschylus, our Aristophanes, and from classics class knew Aristotle had had a couple good ideas, but this wasn't one of them, and it was miles from Modern.

This was 1969. Nixon said we were not bombing Cambodia; he was not a crook. Spiro Agnew, at the cutting Republican intellectual edge, was cutting deals in Maryland. Black Panthers and Weathermen were sentenced in the courtrooms and in the streets— Eldridge Cleaver's soul was on ice. In no time, the National Guard would be shooting students on campus in Middle America, and nothing would be found in Larry O'Brien's office. Moreover, Cleaver's radical philosophy, grounded in Logical Positivism and Pragmatism, based in Emotivist Ethical Theory, would desert him in old age in favor of fashion design and that Old-Time Religion. No one postulated that we'd all have haircuts, Hondas, and mutual funds given enough time and changes of administration. Where did we go?

If, and only if, we examine the ashes of our omission, our pressed white shirts, the defeated tenderness of revolt, the dark matter spinning mutely away in our brains, is there a possibility something might sift out with a little left-over gravity and light. Otherwise, we are confounded by the daily attrition and deconstruction of our molecules, our resistance to meaning vis-a-vis the necessary atomic structures and synthesis of neurons, which finally, or slowly, or eventually give way to nothing, much the way clouds dissolve into the unrehearsed blue, the patchwork sky which contains every atom of our breath and suppositions, the sky which is itself moved around by invisible and unreliable forces, and beneath which, 40 years subsequent, we are still receiving unverified reports of the ballots from Florida, the war in Iraq, and the increasing production costs of oil from a scripted Fox News party line no one will repudiate any time soon enough. Everyone lies. I guess there is still some Wittgenstein in that?

I vaguely remember Kierkegaard saying life can only be understood looking backwards, but it must be lived going forward. Who knew? It's too late now. Winds drift through a pasture where once there was a chestnut mare and an old white cart horse, a couple apple trees—a place with a pond on the edge of nowhere, where eventually beyond all belief, you'd give anything to stand again, to sit in the grass looking at sun edge the salt white clouds, wondering well into middle age what sure use ever to put your mind to....

My 25th Guggenheim Application

I'm nothing, if not persistent. I still want to save the whales, and baby seals, even the battery chickens. America never got a good 5¢ cigar. And I never lived in NYC, though I ate lunch there a time or two. I know New Formalists in high places, but can't escape the ranks of the politically expendable, the plain ignorable. "We don't do business with people we don't do business with." I needed Burt Lancaster to write for me from Atlantic City.

My books come back still shrink-wrapped, thrown through the hopeless window. I command enough romance languages to sweet talk my way through a menu at restaurants where I have to put it on the VISA card, the "Never-Never," as the Brits have it. With the passing of time, and money into the appropriate hands, some of my friends have even turned into Republicans, joined the Knights of Columbus, and they won't share the secret handshake. Some drive pick-up trucks that cost as much as Cadillacs—some drive pick-ups that *are* Cadillacs. They are no help to me or anyone. In this they resemble my relatives.

I don't deserve a MacArthur; I'm not a genius—I don't know the right people. I'm not going to The Club, not lifting a Manhattan and crustless sandwich off a silver tray. And despite poetry's diminishing returns, I continue to be confused with the Christopher Buckley from Yale, the one who writes snappy bits for *Esquire* and *TV Guide*, the guy with the Smoking movie, with the famous father just to the right of Hammurabi. I was called to be on the *Today Show* to chat about my speech writing for George Bush the First—I declined, and they figured I was just trying to leverage a higher fee—it's business. I could have shown up and given the network pundits premature ventricular contractions with my views on Late Capitalism, but the other Buckley is tall and blond, has a blue blazer and entourage, and I'd have seen a check for my expenses about the time Haiti freezes over—but given Global Warming, perhaps I should have given it a shot…. Political currency. That's what I need. "It Takes Money to Make Money"—inscribed over the gate as they turned for a last look at Eden.

I've got a day job, have stood with my hand raised and not lost my place in line. When the phone doesn't ring, it's Oprah, living only a few streets over from where I grew up in Montecito. As for career fulfillment, I remember Lee Trevino BBQd by a bolt of lightning while out there on the job—how hard or long he'd worked had nothing to do with it. He said the next time the weather went south, he'd hold up a 1-iron as even God can't hit a 1-iron. Lee and I share some views on administrators, and like him, I've worked regular hours and tried to keep my head down, I've paid attention to the risk/reward ratio, though he's lined up a few more endorsements than I have.

By the time I was invited to read at the Dodge Festival in New Jersey, Bill Moyers was long gone—another missed opportunity for TV fame and fortune. And the reading wasn't in the big main tent. My pal Len and I were two hundred yards south, off in the woods, a left turn past the port-o-potties, in the clearing with the splintery folding chairs. But on the ride back to the hotel, I shared a van with Yehuda Amichai, who was happy to talk with me though he knew me from no one. His poems risked everything in front of God, and in their modesty, their rough grace and gravity, he had the poverty of our bones almost glowing. He'd been through war, and love, worn the gloves of the dead, and still he had a little hope to share. He could tell I knew his work, and he had a smile for me despite the unopened *Selected* I asked him to sign. The only application he had pending was for more time to write and walk among the garden. He didn't beg.

Oil, Nostalgia, Immigration Reform, & the Decline of the West

All right, geniuses, what do you expect? The Texaco filling station attendants who snapped-to in their white uniforms, caps, and bow ties on *Milton Berle's Texaco Star Theater* are long gone—no one's going to wash your windshield, smiling as they check your tire pressure and oil. No trickle-down economics will bring back that '50s quartet harmonizing "We are the Men of Texaco, We work from Maine to Mexico" as they pump Fire Chief into the tank of your Hummer. You've been carrying home MTBE on your hands for years now and paying ten times as much as you used to for the privilege. Checked the rising rate of autism lately? Your portfolio manager tells you the answer is to buy more Exxon/ Mobile stock. 76 Union had to scrape away half the town of Avila Bay and dump the oil-leached earth into someone else's back yard.

News Flash: Orange County chapters of The Young Republicans are not lining up for work in kitchens San Diego to L.A., or for five bucks an hour under the table shoveling out the stables at Santa Anita, Del Mar, and Hollywood Park. Congress men & women drink year round at the public trough—health care, franking privileges, airline tickets, all on the house. Over half of them on the Hill still like Ike, and can remember most of what Reagan forgot.

They're not turning away troops of Boy Scouts from the strawberry fields around Santa Maria. Some poor SOBs spend 60 hours a week with their backs bent in ditches so we can go to Vons and buy something for an attractive desert. Where did they hide the ballots in Florida? Enron ricocheted 40 billion from California in an energy scheme, Schwartzenegger poaches two billion from kids in classrooms, Carl Rove scripts the White House leaks, the earth is at its hottest in 400 years, and you have this problem with The Law!? With undocumented people mowing lawns, cleaning out your restrooms?

We're not in Brooklyn anymore—this is no black & white Bing Crosby film from the '40s where the worst thing anyone can say is, "Hey, Mac, what's the big idea?"or "Sorry Bud, no dice" just before the millionaire donates his new building to the nuns. Back in the day Cisco & Pancho actually put the *bandidos* in jail, took no kick-backs or percentage off the top. The Mexicans were here before us and Standard Oil.

And who made a bundle off Jimmy Durante on the *Colgate Comedy Hour*, the "great schnozzola," who sang "Smile," "Make Someone Happy," and "Inka Dinka Doo," who was not a language poet, who told the truth in his baggy suit, who never got credit—or cash—for his song writing? Each week he stepped back in black & white into the diminishing spot lights saying good night to Mrs. Calabash, doffing a forlorn fedora to honest inspiration. Who was it who said, "You've Gotta Have Heart"..."Wide as the ocean, deep as the sea"? Not the shareholders, not the board members of the executive committee, not the CFO of the Catholic Church. Every *saludo* and ticket stub of good will expired, unredeemable as Avila Bay dirt.

Instead of a six-shooter, they're using Supply & Demand when you fill up, and, if you buy that explanation, I do have a bridge in Brooklyn.... No one's left who'll say, Howdy, partner, sit and rest a spell. Make yourself at home, Have a cigar, How are you fixed for dough, or, Step right up Sonny Boy, Have one on me. Whatever happened to So Long? Stay tuned? and Yours Truly?

Politicians, administrators, CEOs, I'll trust them as far as I can throw a house, when cows can fly. Never in a million years—that'll be the day. Fold it five ways and put it where the sun don't shine...twice on Sunday. Whatever spin they put on it, I'll bet you dollars to donuts there's not a snowball's chance in hell any of them will put the planet in front of profits.

If there is a God, a God of vengeance that all the red states thump the dust from their Bibles for, leave your number on his pager because He's not picking up. Thanks for nothing, sucker. And, Same to you!

Infinity

Everything is formless where the waves break into the sky, rain and the unremarkable unraveling of the sea. And still the air in shambles. Any oncologist knows you are four times more likely to contract cancer living in L.A. The elementary machinery of salt gave us early warnings up the coast as I J-Waxed the pits from the chrome on my '59 Bel Air. No one was praying for the ocean then.

The taxonomy of pathos dissipates in no time over drinks, the poor reproving nothing, come quarterly dividends. The drug conglomerates won't even look at ALS; not enough of us die annually to make it profitable. The President is going to Mars.

Wind blows its madness and whitecaps off shore. Around the fast food dumpsters, gulls implement late capitalism—I got mine, how'd you make out? Ah, the white, Chamber-of-Commerce ranchitas of the clouds. Come on—the soul looks out on dust.

Yes, I'm not doing anything for lunch. A few years into my last loneliness, my surviving vices are marginal at worst, and I know enough to mistrust the sweetness of the world. The stars, grey as ever, are redundant from here. They burn their way into the past, though we discovered that only recently. Sure, the waves are tipped with light— stars washing away in the tide.

Nevertheless, I came to touch the sea, to feel its afterthoughts evaporate from my fingers…. Infinity has always driven me up a wall. The white dinner plate of the moon, the invisible veil of star dust drifting down—it's all beyond us. I can no more start a new life than that dog who streaked out like a comet from the wide empty fields along Hwy 41 in front of my silver rent-a-car. The white stars of his teeth, the dull sticks of the belly and leg blasting away to the dark hovering forever there at the roadside's edge—its poor bright blood sinking back to salt, to water, to a spume of atoms far from any sea we know.

Inertia / Global Warming

what goes around, comes around…

Before Copernicus, conventional wisdom held that the earth couldn't possibly be moving, turning—or else everything would be torn to pieces…clouds would be ripped from the sky, a ball dropped toward the ground would miss its mark as the earth rotated past. And though Copernicus proved the sun was at the center, and the planets spun around it, most of the thinking, like a body at rest, resisted change.

Giordano Bruno saw other worlds spinning out there and went to the fires for his new age beliefs. His statue still stands in the Campo dei Fiori in Rome where he was burned by The Inquisition, where nothing in that dim firmament has moved for centuries.

Still, some maintain, there is hope. And if we look at hope as a pair of shoes—with holes, without holes—what else is there for it but to put a foot down and walk the unmarked road? The sky cannot help, humming its nostalgic, absentminded tune. Push your hypothetical cart along, your market projections—a cloud is a cup of ashes spilling across the miserable skies.

Take the deposition of the stars—just 4% of the universe is matter, atoms recycled to make us up, and in most quarters five will get you ten that it's the result of a dazzling cosmic crapshoot. As unlikely a shore as this is, every bit of luck, bad or good, washes up here, and we refuse to blame ourselves as we rest our backs against a palm—appreciating how cypresses have gradually considered the wind, expecting to arrive at a resolution beyond an inward galactic tumbling predicted by the focus group.

If God did set every molecule pin-balling about, how improvident it is to sit still and not prize the earth above all else, even if we did walk out of the sea one day on our own two fins with all the applied forces of desire, the impetus to breathe the blue compounds of oxygen just then rolling in from the deckled edge of space?

Endowed Chairs in Business Administration, Doctors of Divinity, God doesn't care how much we finally understand, how much sleep we lose, how many dead stars continue to reach us with their blank checks of light. We lied about the world. We ate our bread.

The quail that orbit my lawn in the sun outshine every rationalization for a gross national product, outsourcing, and foreign trade agreements the corporate think-tanks have cooked up. Despite the primary exports of Panama, Ecuador, and Tierra del Fuego, every observation says it all revolves around us.

The oceans hold their place beneath the drift-net of darkness, sea foam and moon flakes slip through heaven's sieve, through our hands.... Stepping off the plane at LAX, all I have to declare is the Milky Way, the stardust of my brain lost or soon to be lost in the brown heat, the seas working out their last equations of rain.

Ecology & Self Pity at Arroyo Burro Beach

No one at the beach—patch of mist, stick figure in the distance, reeling in a red detergent bottle from the surf.

Another seal's hauled himself out heavily into the air—lines scarred across its skin like ideograms of the natives here who went into the mountains in despair after the Russians and Spanish came, who were never translated, except in the granite-colored clouds holding the lost code of their grief.

Beneath your skin, blood carries the stardust to your brain, each grain lost or soon to be lost, and no sense made of the creek's end here—seaweed, pathos, it's all the same along the sand.

Unlike you, the sky has plenty of time to follow its aimless thoughts. You've come to study at the sea again, and shuffle along wondering if the past is finally past, all the philosophies so many dry leaves blown along the path edging the parking lot.

It will be quiet at the little tables, and you can sit with a glass of something before the fog and general aggravation of the crowd arriving after work. You don't have to think about work, but you do…anymore, it matters only to speak directly, and not dodge about the edges like the plovers, legs flitting back and forth in front of the tide. You have nothing at all to say, but you want to say it anyway. You praise the essential project of your breath, the answer to, What's left?

On the cliff, pampas plumes reach for every particle and wave of light as if they were hard-nosed evidence of the soul. Grey outline of the air, salt displayed upon the wind, white caps—nostalgia for the infinite is all that will be left of us one day.

For now, you are here, in the lenient dusk of October, regions of memory like the marine layer vaguely edging in, recalling friends, the boat of an old Chevy Bel Air that brought you here each day faithfully after school, that sense of hope God took away with middle age.

Another glass, red as the sun, palm leaves catching against the horizon. The stars starting up out of nowhere. Despite the centuries yawning, all the astrological folderol, you know the stars are not spinning out there for you.

Time for coffee now—you might add a teaspoon of astonishment had one lemon grove survived developers. Still, looking west, you think almost all our self-pity could be contained by the sea, had we not been so indolent, had we not already thrown so much into it....

Ineffable

My wife tells me that in thinking of all that might be out there, or is there, seen and un-, our brains comprehend as much about the universe, (or multi-verses), p-branes and M-theory, 11-dimensional Superstrings vis-à-vis the four flat dimensions we're sure we do see, the galaxies red-shifted and taking the A train toward The Great Attractor, and *ad infinitum* re the pre-masticated cosmology books I read before I turn the lamp out and drift off to sleep—in short, every new, salient, and expansive fact or supposition I unearth with the support of some Sauvignon Blanc poured over a moon-white ice cube or two—that we understand as much of the unqualifiable cosmos as our cats—Cecil and Lizzie—do of the world outside our fenced yard where they are never allowed to go.

I remember the nuns in grammar school telling a handful of us in back that we weren't going anywhere if we could not get the new Set-Theory Algebra they'd unloaded on us in 8th grade. (They had abandoned the old Saving Your Immortal Soul theme in favor of the current cutting-edge curriculum for which they'd sacrificed their summer, and so were hammering our poor thick heads with intangible equations to get us graduated and out the door, where we'd be someone else's problem, floating in our dull orbits a city or two away, which at the end of the '50s might as well have been light years, a year itself a longer string of time than any of us could fully comprehend.) I just sat there looking out the huge windows at the sky spinning above the acacia trees, knowing that I preferred the unexamined and intuitive efforts of the clouds to most things on earth. I'd still travel like that if I could.

Fifty years later, no one is close to calculating where all that time has actually gone, except perhaps Einstein, and reliable reports say he didn't like doing the math and showing his work any more than we did; he just worked most of it out in his head. His notion of curved space-time saying it could all circle back on us, might well explain the big invisible picture, but it also sounds vaguely religious. I think of the clouds just continuing around the earth, "continuing" being the key word there. Yet Einstein's idea does extrapolate Supergravity, and that clarifies for some how the energy of a large number of particles curves the universe or forms a bound state, like a black hole, inside which, they say, time comes to an end. But let's not go there.

My cats in their comfortable middle age are content lying on the wide, cool, afternoon lawn, content with the lizards some infinite force has darting occasionally before them in the light; they no longer give a thought to the mesh along the top of the fence that holds them here. Still, I look out at night, at what I once described as the barbed-wire of stars, but there's no limit now and that guess does not fill in any blanks. There is a wonderful photo of Einstein riding a bicycle around his driveway in Princeton; he's wearing a sweater, vest, and tie, his shoes are shined, but he's grinning for all he's worth, having just escaped (I still remember the look) from school into the enormous freedom of the air.

It's difficult to travel anywhere these days since we have the cats. They depend on us for a reliable interpretation of experience and a variety of cuisine. My wife says she just hopes we can get back to Italy one day, now that we can finally afford that gondola ride in Venice— that black hole of tourist budgets. A little travel, one hopeful dimension that appears to be *effable* re: our remaining years. (*Effable*—a word that is only part of a word sliding down the time line, Latin to Old French to Middle English, a verb we should—in a perfect world—be able to use, as our friend Bill liked to pun) whereas all beyond here is dark and *ineffable*, tied inescapably to every last thing we will never be sure about.

Mitochondrial

hasta darnos la suma
de la totalidad de
infinito… —Pablo Neruda

The wind may still be outside the Arlington Theater, holding my coat after the Saturday matinee—I forget exactly where I left it—but everything adds up eventually somehow, according to atomic theory… invisible losses, that never reach the page, losses nonetheless….

At night, I hear the coyotes on the mesa, last of the romantics, howling, *Love, Love, Oh Careless Love*, whether there's a moon or not. I lie awake, the lost days out there where the stars gather and graze in the blue night, over the foothills, where I've lost my way back forever.

I recognize half a dozen clouds that have tracked me down with that vague grey weight from childhood. Clouds improvise and it's hard to tell, but I know them. And the stars, strung across the night like chicken wire, though moving away from us, aren't going anywhere.

I want to say the eucalyptus trees consider the wind a necessary annoyance, an outright provocation, but I'm projecting—I just like to say things and hope they add up. Half of everyone's interested in Jello-wrestling and *Survivor*, though there may not be as direct a connection as first appears. Most are not so much interested in infinity, and so are unwittingly Zen, in the moment—often in life insurance or debt consolidation, investments in Assisted Living in Indiana. If you make all your payments on time you do not have to worry about parallel universes.

In California, honey bees are literally disappearing into the blue—lost, dying, and it might be cell phone signals crisscrossing and interrupting their homing radar—or a virus—default biology. The farmers and those of us that eat are worried about pollination, the lack thereof, the road to rock, sand, our witless ruin, and Riverside where there is always drought.

Some still believe crop circles are extra terrestrial—not due to the British blokes who admitted to having everyone on. There are still votes for animal gods, and one god that covers everything with seven orthodox days of intelligent design. Pick any leaf and it's more complicated than that.

Everything happens because of what you did before, but this is just cellular degeneration, planned obsolescence, not reincarnation, not a reason why we're here. Not another *Jeopardy* question about the CERN particle accelerator—is it in France or Switzerland? The positrons collide on the border, but that doesn't tell us where the clouds go. I'm always looking southeast at the sea. Like everything, clouds probably keep circling here, changing into our breath, working along in formation in our blood from thousands of millions years back, where the scientists think the mitochondrial DNA hopped off a comet and got in the swim.

The nuclear quotient and codes from interloping bacteria slowly, gradually accounted for us, our bright and promising futures, and eventually for me walking down the hall in the middle of the night wondering where I'm going…back to bed…and soon I'm walking past the old storefronts downtown on State Street, the Woolworth's turned to a bookstore, to sporting goods, to a café. But it's the same gilt-edged glass that caught and released my image, age 5, tagging along with mother to the shops.

The windows do the same today, in a million specks of light, my grey image imprinted on the sky, which may be all we have when it comes to the sum total of infinity.

Dispatch from the Garden at 57

I love the red-winged blackbirds taking their places on the phone lines for the falling light. And the squads of crows rowing home out of the far blue after a day in the broccoli and artichoke fields—I love them and all that high, unheard music, the intuitive cantatas slip-streaming along up there. If I look back past the canyons sunk off shore, past the plates of shale cantilevered against the sky, even past the two royal palms reaching up from this mesa—rustling, tilting back and forth with their invisible knowledge—what deeper realizations really await me?

So I praise the purple bottlebrush, my bed of double delight roses, the thick, rouged cheek of late afternoon. I love each deep breath I take here, away from everything, love looking up along side the pomegranates and pittosporum, the ornamental plum—one more thing still breathing. I love the yellow grass of January I don't have to mow, and the self-sufficient sandstone hills, life still at every turn as the bronzed atmosphere mists down.

The sky glazes over with opalescent clouds, and my cat, Cecil B., charges across the yard after shadows and the come-ons of gusts among the weeds. I fan my fingers like the sheet music of the light, I think a little about a poem escaping on the air. I pick up my dialogue with the hard-skinned lemon tree and do not worry about the wind, the separation of clouds and bones, the smoke drifting away like my aspirations.... I'm lighting up my last *Cubano*—a *Romeo y Julieta* my student gave me, hand delivered by his father from the island—I'm celebrating with an Italian bar glass full of double-wood single malt, a gift from my old friend, a Chicano who lives up the street—somehow, even back of beyond in Lompoc, there's an almost international atmosphere today.

But it's cold for California. The humming birds have gone south, far, I'm sure, past Santa Barbara where no one can now afford to live. I throw on my grey-blue Rugby shirt and thus match the winter light wearing thin over the west, shining like the knees on my good pair of slacks. It's a Ralph Lauren Polo, $2.95 at the Salvation Army Thrift—Rugby and Polo, two sports I've just recently given up. But the shirt fits, and so I wear it—pride and irony dispersed in equal parts when you can afford not to ask, How Much?

You hit plateaus in life, you think you know things—but at any level, there's been no salvation in sight. And, given a liberal arts education, when I think of how I might improve my station in life, Aristotle comes to mind—how, puzzled by the inexplicable current off the coast of Boeotia, he jumped into the swirling water for enlightenment; or Empedocles, who, nearing death and wanting to be thought a god, vanished into thin air by throwing himself into the fires of Mt. Etna. There are, however, some things self-defeating with regard to career.

Like Cecil, I've adjusted to the friendly confines of Lompoc. He loves the inexpensive brand of Chicken Feast and at 16+ pounds could care less about irony. When he's cleaned his plate, he just wants out the front for a punch-up with whoever has it coming, a pursuit which, more often than not, damages advancement—I let a thought about work and department politics dissipate. I'd give him a dram of my single malt if it would calm him—it works for me in the twilight these days. For now, he's content on the chaise longue, keeping me company on my birthday. My wife is at Yoga class, and I again assume the position, Sea Lion at Rest. I have salmon filet and yellow squash for dinner, but no cake, not a crumb of carbohydrate—on this diet over a year now, everything I try works as well as prayer.....

Fifty-seven today. Firing up this *puro* and watching the smoke drift heavenward, the starry flow chart unfurl, still unreadable. Today, it's inconsequential that I am older by a year than yesterday—always, there are the same number of bricks to hoist up hill. Still, no matter what God's left unfinished, I've done my work. So I'll leave everything to the sea that, like a bill collector, is never far from my door—the dark sea, where today, alone or not, I've decided I will be happy, drifting in the small boat of my heart.

After a Theme by Vallejo, After a Theme by Justice

for Jon Veinberg

It will come for me in Florence with the evening light, and on account of the light, in early autumn before the rainstorms have arrived—when the *sfumato*, that smoke of rose and saffron, has so overrun the air that my worn heart, poor moth, will want to take up after the profligate clouds, their violet sinking toward the west. It will find me, once more extending my stay for no reason beyond the light, known far too well by the *vinaios*, in the little places for soup—on a day when I am little more than another narrow shadow on Borgo Santi Apostoli or Via della Terme, my body dependent on a stick, but I will not be tired of this, for even though my shoulders press against the brick, and I have no clue, my eyes will be at attention, thinking that the road is still ahead.

Doubtless a Sunday with its poor excuses for an afternoon—the trattorias dark, the tourist couples gone from the goldsmiths' shops on the Ponte Vecchio. A Sunday like all the others when I've made my way early to the loggia for the open sun in the fountain, to sit again and admire the statues, those palpable, undiminished shapes, and that smooth, colossal beauty in marble-perfect clouds that saunter down each noon from Fiesole—both reminding us of a life surpassing our own, both headed one way or the other in time. And what will it matter then if I have a smoke, comforted as I will be by the company of these white choirs of air and stone, their long and brilliant reflection on it all. And earlier, at that point where the standard-bearing cart halted on its way back from battle, I will have stopped in the mercato, and out of respect, and again for luck, I'll have rubbed the bronze snout of the *Porcillino*.

Then, I will make my way by heart to the Baptistry where the symbolism of black marble pressed alongside white will not have escaped me, where I will admire once more Ghiberti's self portrait among the panels, the bald humility of his head there on the Gates of Paradise, and looking much the same, I'll envy him his dull, protracted shining. And the sun will be bright then in the camera lenses of tourists, as atop the Duomo they focus toward Giotto's Campanile—the white, green, and terra cotta marbles blanching in that aureate stream, and the shade sliding down Ghiberti's burnished doors, and the tales about this world will once more be old tales, still lacking a little in perspective just like the blue above me when it's stripped down to a red flaming along the roofs and river banks, when the surface of the Arno is brazed for an hour or so with gold, as I head up the hillside to my room in the *soggiorno*. There, I'll finally lean across the window sill and not step aside as the far clouds fade along that road on which each of us is at last alone. And I might think then of Michelangelo at ninety despairing of all the world, of all his great art, flayed as he was with God, with the knotted ropes, the sticks of time; and for a moment I, too, might think, unwittingly, that I've seen it all.

But then I may well recall my friend in a place as strange and far away as Fresno, too old, after all, to know any better than to ride his bicycle recklessly on sidewalks by the thrift shops and Basque hotels, trying the patience of folks at the fruit stands and used-book stalls, smiling his great Baltic teeth at no one he recognizes any more, pedaling slowly home past the one revival theater still showing films in black and white. I think I'll be able to picture it as he puts his feet up on his front porch, and though he's sworn it off, he'll pour himself a water glass of wine red as an autumn sun burning low through the sycamores, and for no reason better than the end of another day, he'll drink to a deep and cloudless sky.

Gravity Waves

for Jack Gilbert

Years back, a former student wrote saying he was in a writers group in San Francisco with you. That's as close as we've ever come—different orbits, however many removes…but I had to wonder how low-in-the-bones-lonely you must have been to sit with locals and beginners, and how modest, given the lean tolerances, the spare way you see a line. I think of rocks in those hand-wedged walls in Greece or Spain, how you gave up the accolades and escaped the hoopla of New York, hung the artifice, the glitter. It seemed you required little outside yourself, but always the whirlpool of the heart, the wondering about what might be coming still, side-door through the dark….

Along those lines, I've picked up a book on gravity waves—scientists with desk-sized aluminum bars seining for radiation, gravitational rim-shots from supernovas and black holes, expecting the bars to ring when they detect a delicate, low key stellar meter. But so far, they say, in studying the sky, we've been watching a silent movie. A hundred years later, we haven't heard a thing.

But when I pick up your books, I can feel the thread-tight ricochet off the stanzas, that kind of burning that goes at least as far as the soul's white flame, and plenty of ash to sift through for those who give a damn, those who've spent their salt and blood. Same gravel, same dust, and what's transmuted beyond that? Here are my warmed-over ideas, shared long-distance, dressed up like a dog's dinner; here I am with my soul's tin can, its make-do string out the window to the night sky waiting for the stars to sing back their fused strophes—all these elliptical, spiral, beer-barreled galaxies, pushed and pulled by the invisible, spinning away from us. But it's not about stars, not here with our lonely brains, with flowers and our momentary distillation of atoms, our longing to be more than the sum of the parts for the few freeze frames we're able to sit in.

I remember the '50s and Humphrey Road, my first Schwinn bike, the blue roofs of the resort bungalows by the beach, the whole universe just beyond Miramar Point where the sea reached into the air. In 1986 I saw a comet there I will not see again, and was grateful for a while for my life despite the ice and dust of everything fizzing away—the sands of heaven sprayed here and there across the straightedge of space, the clouds going nowhere finally in an unconscious loop. They tell us that the future is always the thing, but I don't feel I ever get there.

What dominion remains when we have lost an appetite for God? Isn't the root of all unhappiness our desire for things, for which, with little question, we find ourselves eternally deserving? 2/3ds of the world can't manage a cheese sandwich and the Vice-President is off shooting quail in the name of justice and the minimum wage. Not that God gives a fig about our anguish or the no-bid selling off of the Republic. As much as the next man, I'd like to call for my pipe, my bowl, my fiddlers three, and once in a while, when it's convenient, think I know what God wants when I have a choice to make between the inside track on an IPO and what that populist Plato called The Good For Man. Sorrow arrives on a horse cart or in a flop-top Cadillac. Play ball or get a parade in Dallas. Follow the money. Do what we will, the trees agree on the increasing indigence of the air, but where can they turn for restitution? If there were angels, would the planet be losing a space twice the size of Paris every day to deforestation? Something is on its way.

I'm a ways behind you, not 60 yet, not yet looking squarely at the exit. The sea is still there where it was when I was a boy, and without too much time or difficulty I can walk there, and live with the blind inevitability, its deteriorating text. Standing before waves, I always hoped there was a God, but metaphysically these days, I look to my cats for comforts, for any intimation of what was first, what came next. And are we even half as good as they think we are? So it seems sweet and reasonable to praise, at this late date, a little emptiness, the possibility that something may come to fill it, and that would mean we did not go begging all our days, hanging like a single shirt on the line, hands raised, no defense against the implacable all about us.

About the universe, Jack, well, we can still hear the fossil whisper of the Big Bang, the microwave radiation in the rocks—what can we do with that? But given all that is invisible, all that is kept from us in the wind, shot through the black vacuum and happenstance, rubbing two sticks together will serve you better on a cold night. Yet those on the cutting edge are worrying about gravity waves, membrane theory the eleventh dimension. They are done with dark matter now and even dark energy, some details of which you probably recall from winter afternoons, standing on the curb of Highland Ave., waiting for the streetcar as clouds of coal dust and snow orbited Pittsburgh and settled in. No matter what we formulate, we spend our lives here in hope, or in refusing it. Since they've proved that time and space are one in the same, we'd better stop looking into the sky and get on with it here on earth, even though we could well just be waiting for the next thing to hit us.

Turning 59

Now I can nag the stars with impunity, because, Why Not? It's still a one-sided conversation and I don't know much more than I ever did, except that nothing's going to change at this point beyond our planned obsolescence? The Metaphysician as Motor City CEO....

So, whether I poke my walking stick in the face of creation, or cuss a blue streak across the sky, or not, what will be, will be—as that great American poet Doris Day sang when I was 7. I didn't much believe it then, thinking I could exert my will in the neighborhood by raising the loudest ruckus. But given all the people I've loved who have died since—despite my objections in the strongest possible terms—I guess I believe it now.

Though not so well that I'm anything like a Zen scholar, or have learned to manage my blood pressure as the President's corporate gangs plunder the planet selling-off the remaining bits. I understand a couple things by now. Haven't I read the layman's handbook on parallel universes and Super String Theory trying to get a handle on part of it? But that only explains why things seem always to be in a knot, and why you have to do everything at least twice to get anywhere—conclusions I'd come to long ago working in academia. So where does that leave me now?

Well, there's always Aristotle, who lost his currency for me in the '60s when we hit the streets thinking we could stop the war and restore the Republic. But catharsis—that rings a certain temple bell, calling the cosmic order to account with curses and splenetic rants, especially if you're standing by the sea and page through the great blind book of folly pealed off a wave at a time. You can hurl your most recent reproof at the pinpoints of light overhead that likely add up to nothing more than pinpoints of light, if space-time bends back into itself like a huge brioche as Einstein, Hawking and others surmise. In which case, what earthly good is any theory, all of it so hypothetically referential, explicable as the first, essential equation of the dark.

At least the clouds are not dead yet and so there's still material with which to work in my metaphysical dotage. The only way to the proof is through the EXIT—like all the principals at the end of *Hamlet* strewn across the bloody stage—an outcome that will not in the short run advance your station in life—all the physics at work, visibly and invisibly, strategically opposed to your extended stay on this mortal coil. Many happy returns, as they say....

My cats love me. About my age in cat years, they don't know they are going to die, and I'm not about to tell them. It's hard to come by cheerful company. This summer, I'm sitting in the shade of our pine tree between 5:00 and 7:00—a skill mastered in my advancing years—and remembering my grandparents in Kentucky who valued such character building activities, who were, for as long as I could remember, as comfortable as clouds, and who slipped off up there somewhere one day in my hazy youth when I wasn't paying attention. In their memory, in memory of the sky that lets me breathe, I'm going to raise a glass of well-structured, fruit-forward Spanish wine—a dark one from Zaragosa I can afford now—as the late implacable light contents itself against the house side, yellow and rich as a French, soft-ripened cheese. I'll follow the shadowy fingers of the pine from west to east, and one or two paper-white clouds, as frayed around the edges as hope, sailing slowly by—clouds that have been circling the globe since I first spied them as a boy sashaying out there above the surf at Miramar beach where I knew every rock and barnacle bequeathed by the sea to me and the creatures of the tide. What's to be lost in naming names even though the whole Midwest might not know one beach from another here? Why not recount all I love, praise the salt canticle of the air in those slow days and cite such riches as are left me beneath the benign oversight of the palms?

Why not walk out to the balcony as the night comes set in Lompoc, the back of beyond? No reason remains not to pull myself up to full height and run out the usual objections—puzzled and profane as ever—to the stars, that know my limits as well as I do, the gravity and ephemeral delight, the full extent of my unresolved, unanchored time and space.

I've been to the cafés on Montparnasse, eaten the intellectual shellfish from the pyramid of ice, sipped the dry Entre-deux-Mers, and to no one's surprise, Robbe-Grillet never showed. In Barcelona, at Los Caracoles, I sat beneath the signed photo of Sacha Distel—and it was much the same. I visited Modigliani's grave, a dull slab among a field of 100 dull slabs—I was 36—the inference of the winter sky was clear.

In the caves of Altamira, the red bison and spotted deer, the sprayed outlines of a hand from 150 thousand years ago are the same ones that appear with the bushman in South Africa only 200 years back—same cerebral stratospheres, same starry exhalation against the walls.

Sixty next. No escaping the rest of it. I'm writing a few rambling poems that I like, circulating out here in the provinces. And from Cézanne I learned—never forget where you're from on earth. He quit Paris, went home to find the true life of light in three panes of color. He painted one mountain more than sixty times and loved a pine tree from his boyhood to abstraction. At the end, bad legs, diabetes, eyes losing focus, he saw nonetheless how one thing overlays the next in the sun, in the burning blue; he saw his valley 100 different ways, in color harmonies and the unsolvable geometries of the heart—and at last distilled it all to brush strokes that take us up into the sky…usually a cloud there representing something, as long as we have a minute to step outside and look.

Acknowledgments

Artful Dodge	—	Productivity
Askew	—	The Semiotics of Ham & Cheese; Inertia/Global Warming
Basalt	—	Beginning with a Line by Tu Fu
Calapooya	—	The Ponies At Chincoteague
Cimarron Review	—	Ars Vita
5 AM	—	Paris Dispatch; Time Change
Green Mountains Review	—	Modern History
Hotel Amerika	—	My History of Ancient Egypt; The Sea Again; Mitochondrial; Ecology & Self Pity at Arroyo Burro Beach
New England Review/Bread Loaf Quarterly	—	After a Theme by Vallejo, After a Theme by Justice
Northeast Corridor	—	Les Etoiles
Paragraph	—	There
The Prose Poem: An International Journal	—	Ignis Fatuus
Rattle	—	After a Reading, Charles Bukowski Returns …
Rivendell	—	Dispatch from Santa Barbara
Salt Hill	—	Dispatch from the Garden at 57; Buckley y yo; Turning 59
Santa Barbara Review	—	There & Then
Santa Monica Review	—	Time In The World
Sentence	—	Eternity; Conspiracy Theory: Low Carb Diet Conversion; Infinity; My 25th Guggenheim Application; Gravity Waves
Snake Nation Review	—	Spring Sabbatical; Humility
Talking River Review	—	Guardian Angel
Vs.	—	The Assoc. Professor Crashes the Awards Program at the National Arts Club
Whirligig	—	Last Days of the Hot Rod Kids

My deepest gratitude to the John Simon Guggenheim Memorial Foundation for a Fellowship in Poetry for 2007-2008 which provided time for the final editing and revision of this book.

Find These Uncommonly Good Tupelo Press Books
at tupelopress.org or call 802-366-8185

On Dream Street	(2007)	Melanie Almeder	$16.95
Animal Gospels	(2006)	Brian Barker	$16.95
The Gathering Eye	(2004)	Tina Barr	$14.95
Mulberry	(2006)	Dan Beachy-Quick	$16.95
Bellini in Istanbul	(2005)	Lillias Bever	$16.95
Cloisters	(2008)	Kristin Bock	$16.95
Sincerest Flatteries	(2007)	Kurt Brown	$ 9.95
Modern History, Prose Poems	(2008)	Christopher Buckley	$16.95
After the Gold Rush	(2006)	Lewis Buzbee	$14.00
The Flammable Bird	(2006)	Elena Karina Byrne	$14.95
Masque	(2007)	Elena Karina Byrne	$16.95
Spill	(2007)	Michael Chitwood	$16.95
Signed, numbered limited edition hardcover*			$100.00
Locket	(2005)	Catherine Daly	$16.95
Psalm	(2007)	Carol Ann Davis	$16.95
Signed, numbered limited edition hardcover*			$100.00
The Flute Ship "Castricum"	(2001)	Amy England	$14.95
Victory & Her Opposites	(2007)	Amy England	$19.95
Duties of the Spirit	(2005)	Patricia Fargnoli	$16.95
Calendars	(2003)	Annie Finch	$14.95 (pb) $22.95 (hc)
Ice, Mouth, Song	(2005)	Rachel Contreni Flynn	$16.95
Mating Season	(2004)	Kate Gale	$16.95
Do The Math	(2008)	Emily Galvin	$16.95
Other Fugitives and Other Strangers	(2006)	Rigoberto Gonzalez	$16.95
No Boundaries	(2003)	Ray Gonzalez, ed	$22.95
Time Lapse	(2003)	Alvin Greenberg	$22.95 (hc)
Keep This Forever	(2008)	Mark Halliday	$16.95
Longing Distance	(2004)	Sarah Hannah	$16.95
Inflorescence	(2007)	Sarah Hannah	$16.95
Numbered limited edition hardcover*			$100.00
Invitaion to a Secret Feast	(2008)	Joumana Haddad	$16.95
Night, Fish, and Charlie Parker	(2006)	Phan Nhien Hao	$16.95
The Next Ancient World	(2001)	Jennifer Michael Hecht	$13.95
A House Waiting for Music	(2003)	David Hernandez	$14.95
Storm Damage	(2002)	Melissa Hotchkiss	$13.95
Red Summer	(2006)	Amaud Jamaul Johnson	$16.95
Dancing in Odessa	(2004)	Ilya Kaminsky	$16.95
The Garden Room	(2006)	Joy Katz	$ 9.95

Abiding Places, Korea North and South	(2006)	Ko Un	$16.95
You Can Tell the Horse Anything	(2004)	Mary Koncel	$16.95
Ardor	(2008)	Karen An Hwei Lee	$16.95
Dismal Rock	(2007)	Davis McCombs	$16.95
Signed, numbered limited edition hardcover*			$100.00
Biogeography	(2008)	Sandra Meek	$16.95
Bright Turquoise Umbrella	(2004)	Hermine Meinhard	$16.95
Why is the Edge Always Windy?	(2005)	Mong Lan	$16.95
Vacationland	(2005)	Ander Monson	$16.95
Miracle Fruit	(2003)	Aimee Nezhukumatathil	$14.95
At the Drive-In Volcano	(2007)	Aimee Nezhukumatathil	$16.95
The Imaginary Poets	(2005)	Alan Michael Parker, ed	$19.95
Everyone Coming Toward You	(2005)	David Petruzelli	$16.95
Darkling	(2001)	Anna Rabinowitz	$14.95
The Wanton Sublime	(2006)	Anna Rabinowitz	$16.95
When the Eye Forms	(2006)	Dwaine Rieves	$16.95
Bend	(2004)	Natasha Sajé	$16.95
Approximately Paradise	(2005)	Floyd Skloot	$16.95
Selected Poems: 1970-2005	(2008)	Floyd Skloot	$17.95
Distant Early Warning	(2005)	Rad Smith	$16.95
O Woolly City	(2007)	Priscilla Sneff	$16.95
Every Bird is One Bird	(2001)	Francine Sterle	$13.95
Nude in Winter	(2006)	Francine Sterle	$16.95
Embyros & Idiots	(2007)	Larissa Szporluk	$16.95
I Want This World	(2001)	Margaret Szumowski	$13.95
The Night of the Lunar Eclipse	(2005)	Margaret Szumowski	$16.95
In the Mynah Bird's Own Words	(2003)	Barbara Tran	$9.95
Devoted Creatures	(2004)	Bill Van Every	$14.95
This Sharpening	(2006)	Ellen Doré Watson	$16.95
The Way Home, A Wilderness Odyssey	(2004)	Bibi Wein	$16.95
Narcissus	(2008)	Cecilia Woloch	$ 9.95
The Making of Collateral Beauty	(2006)	Mark Yakich	$ 9.95
American Linden	(2002)	Matthew Zapruder	$14.95 (pb) $22.95 (hc)

* Proceeds from the purchase of these limited edition books help to support *Poetry in the Schools*, a national initiative that brings working poets into elementary and high schools across the country.